Decolon ~~WITHDRAWN~~

A volume in the
Tom Slick World Peace Series
Lyndon B. Johnson School of Public Affairs

DECOLONIZATION AND WORLD PEACE

by Brian Urquhart

 UNIVERSITY OF TEXAS PRESS, AUSTIN

First edition, 1989

Requests for permission to reproduce material from this
work should be sent to:
  Permissions
  University of Texas Press
  Box 7819
  Austin, Texas 78713-7819

Library of Congress Cataloging-in-Publication Data

Urquhart, Brian.
  Decolonization and world peace / by Brian Urquhart.—
1st ed.
    p. cm.—(Tom Slick world peace series)
  ISBN 0-292-73853-6 (alk. paper).—ISBN 0-292-71559-5
(pbk.: alk. paper)
   1. World politics—1945– 2. Decolonization. I. Title.
II. Series.
D843.U77   1989
909.82—dc20   89-4865
                                       CIP

Contents

Acknowledgments

I am deeply grateful to the Tom Slick Memorial Fund for making it possible for me to give this series of lectures at the University of Texas. In particular I wish to thank Dean Max Sherman of the LBJ School for making the arrangements and the schedule. I greatly appreciate the encouragement and advice I received from him and from former Associate Dean Dagmar Hamilton.

I had the great good fortune, in parallel with my lectures, to share a seminar in the LBJ School with Professor Roger Louis. This was, for me at any rate, a memorable experience which allowed me to enjoy at first hand the superb quality and character both of faculty and of students at the University of Texas. I am also grateful to my friend Professor Standish Meacham for his help and support.

Susan Roush was an invaluable guide and helper. Her capacity for cheerfully solving all problems and answering all questions added greatly to the pleasure of my all-too-brief time at the University of Texas.

Finally, I wish to express my appreciation to President Franklin A. Thomas of the Ford Foundation, at which I am a scholar-in-residence, for providing me with the base and the facilities for my present activities.

Decolonization and World Peace

Introduction

At its beginning in 1945, the United Nations had 50 member states. It was an organization that still reflected a world of empires and colonial systems and the interests of that world. Its concerns were peace in Europe and Asia, clearing up the debris of World War II, and the collective management, under the leadership of the great powers of the day, of threats to the peace or acts of aggression such as those which had given rise to that war. There was little anticipation of the fact that the nature and composition of the international community was about to undergo a radical change. Now, at the end of 1988, the United Nations has 159 member states.

The United States, the twentieth century's leading pioneer in the development of international institutions, was, in 1945, unique among the great powers that were the permanent members of the United Nations Security Council. It was not only by far the richest and most powerful nation in the world. It had itself broken away from colonial domination less than two hundred years before. The United States had a view of the world very different from that of the other great powers in the Security Council.

This American view of the world was to dominate the postwar international scene and to have a radical effect both on reconstruction and on the development of the United Nations—with results not all clearly foreseen by the government of the United States itself. Over forty years later the legacy of this world view—an international community of more than 160 sovereign, independent states, of which a large majority are in the nonaligned or so-called Third World—has hitherto often been a matter more for concern and anxiety than for rejoicing in Washington.

Of the basic concepts underlying both the League of Nations and the United Nations, none was so highly valued by the United States, or indeed was so particularly American, as the principle of self-determination. Only partially applied in 1919 as a criterion for the disposal of the territories of vanquished empires, in 1945 the principle of self-determination was considered to be applicable to *all* colonial possessions. The hope that the process of decolonization would be gradual, systematic and orderly, was soon swept away by a "wind of change" which quickly developed an irresistible force of its own. The process of decolonization was virtually completed within thirty years under an initial impetus from the United States' conviction that decolonization was a logical extension of allied war aims.

The old order—the hegemony of a few great empires—was thus dissolved. According to the United Nations Charter, the new order that was to replace it was a world of sovereign, independent states working together in a system of collective security and responsibility centered in the United Nations. This order was to be supervised, and if necessary enforced, by the leading victors of World War II, the five permanent members of the United Nations Security Council. The Charter, however, having been written well before rapid decolonization began, took little account of the effect of a vastly expanded membership both on the stately procedures outlined in the Charter and on the automatic Western voting majority, which was taken for granted as the natural order in the United Nations in its early years.

The 1945 vision of peace through the United Nations was soon rudely shaken. The onset of East-West ideological conflict, or Cold War, quickly paralyzed the capacity of the new world organization to maintain the peace and to provide the comprehensive security system that might also have made progressive disarmament possible. The revolution of decolonization therefore took place in a near-vacuum of international authority. Newly independent nations, looking to the Security Council in vain for security, increasingly tended to arm themselves and, if necessary, to go it alone in military ventures that usually ended in disaster. There was also a growing temptation to play one superpower off against the other.

Since 1945 the majority of wars, claiming an estimated eighteen million, mostly civilian, casualties, have been fought in the developing world with weapons provided by the industrialized capitalist and socialist worlds. The chaos of war and the burden of arms buying have had a disastrous impact on the capacity of many newly independent countries to come to grips with the tasks of development and growth which their new independent status urgently demanded.

Decolonization and its repercussions have had a major impact on the effort to evolve a system of international order. In the early years, for example, the United States and its Western allies were confronted with frequent Soviet vetoes in the Security Council. They therefore devised the so-called Acheson Plan or "Uniting for Peace" Resolution, which set up a Collective Measures Committee and Peace Observation Commission independent of the Security Council. This plan also sidestepped the Charter by permitting questions blocked by a veto in the Security Council to be transferred by majority vote to the General Assembly, where there was no veto and where the United States controlled an unquestioned automatic majority.

As decolonization picked up speed in the late 1950s, that majority became less reliable. The vote in 1971 to seat the People's Republic of China, a decision which the United States had successfully blocked for twenty-one years, marked dramatically the end of the automatic US majority. The newly independent countries, their sights fixed on economic development and on the completion of decolonization, could not be relied on or manipulated on a number of important issues. The United States and the West thus became disillusioned with the once-favored General Assembly, reverted to the Security Council, and began in their turn to use the veto as a defense against the majority.

The decade of the 1970s was a watershed in the evolution of the United Nations. The former colonial territories which had, since the early 1960s, been taking their place in the United Nations, were a radical, angry constituency. Newly acquired independence had only served to accentuate the bitter frustrations of time lost and opportunities missed. This group of nations was angrily aware that it had been denied the greatest economic boom in human history, the industrial revolution, and strongly resented the economic supremacy of, and exploitation by, the established, profitably industrialized old world.

By the 1970s the honeymoon atmosphere of the early days of decolonization had worn off, and the grim realities of life in an economically competitive world had become apparent to the newly independent countries. The United Nations General Assembly, where they enjoyed a voting majority, seemed the only forum in which they could assert their rights, and a decade of radical rhetoric ensued. The so-called New International Economic Order was one example of such rhetoric, the Zionism-Racism resolution another. Such measures, although powerless to produce any practical effect, were an expression of protest and indignation which created strong repercussions. Ironically, the target of much of this rhetoric tended to be the erstwhile champion of decolonization, the United States.

It would be hard to imagine a more counterproductive course in terms of practical results. The Western industrialized countries were unlikely to respond positively to rhetorical onslaughts, which only gave substance to suspicions that the Third World was an anti-Western, and particularly an anti-American, conspiracy inspired by the Soviet Union. Moreover the Western industrialized countries, which paid an overwhelming proportion of the UN budget, were now being required by large majority votes in the General Assembly to subsidize measures of which they strongly disapproved. Such a development was bound to embitter their attitude to the United Nations and to many of its agencies.

Thus began in the mid-1970s a strong United States reaction against the system of international organizations it had sponsored and so warmly championed at the beginning. The United Nations became identified in Washington as an irresponsible, Third World, quasi-Marxist, anti-American entity, and United States policy in, and toward, international organizations radically changed. A combination of Third World rhetoric, Soviet obstructionism, and an ideological swing to the Neoconservative Right in the United States had caused the principal founding nation of the UN to turn against the organization.

The 1980s have been a testing and frustrating period for the United Nations and for those who believe that in spite of all its failings it is an essential and important organization. The organization never worked well when the international climate was frozen by the Cold War, and its manipulation by the Third World majority and the resulting antagonism of the United States and of other Western governments further hobbled its effectiveness.

There now seems to be a prospect of better and more constructive times ahead. The warming of relations between the US and the USSR has already vastly improved the international climate. Practical cooperation between them on certain regional conflicts has already produced impressive results, notably in southern Africa, and more is to be expected. In this new summer of international relations, the UN has once again come into its own as a peacekeeping, peacemaking organization, to which any nation can come for help without loss of face.

The countries of the Third World have also changed with time. Ideology—especially Marxist economics—appears to have been cast aside, and a far more pragmatic approach to international politics and economics is evident. In the United Nations radical anti-Western and anti-United States rhetoric has been muted, and there seems to be a new determination to use the organization as a forum for cooperation rather than for confrontation.

The new mood of pragmatism and common sense on a broad range of essential problems bodes well for the pressing task of mobilizing collective responsibility for the great global problems—social, economic, and environmental—which now loom larger and larger as the determining factors in the future of the human race.

These changes of attitude may have come just in time for governments to face together the multiplicity of decisions which will determine whether, in the years to come, we travel the road of well-managed progress or the downhill slide to disaster. Decolonization represented, on the international plane, the democratization of the community of nations. The next great step for that community will be to make the right basic choices about the future and to work together to realize them.

The following chapters are based on lectures given at The University of Texas at Austin in the first three months of 1988. Since that time there have been important international developments in several regions of the world. I have adjusted the original texts of the lectures to take account of these developments.

The first chapter deals with the origins and process of decolonization. The next two chapters cover two important episodes of decolonization, the Palestine question and decolonization in Africa. The final chapter comments on the Iran-Iraq War, an episode not directly related to decolonization but illustrative of the problems of dealing with regional conflict in the developing world.

December 31, 1988

1. The Decolonization Process

Tom Slick's dedication of his book, *The Last Great Hope,* conveys in one sentence the message of these lectures. "To the fine world that we can attain under the benefits of peace, if only we have judgment enough to take the right steps to assure peace."[1] I have spent most of my life trying to figure out what those right steps are.

The right steps to assure peace have so far been a rather faltering expedition through the great changes and revolutions of the forty years since World War II. It is important to remember, in thinking about peace or international cooperation or the future, that these forty years have probably been the most revolutionary forty years in human history. We have changed a great deal, and now we have to make a reckoning.

One of the great revolutions of this period has been the process of decolonization, which has completely changed the geopolitical map of the world. It has also changed the conditions under which we seek to assure peace and to develop what we hope will be a more sensible order in the world.

When I was at school during the twenties, the headmaster used to address the whole school every

Tuesday. He had two props in this weekly lecture. One was a map of the world, which showed more than a quarter of its surface marked in red, denoting British possessions. The other was a jingoistic book called *Deeds That Thrilled the Empire*. We were encouraged to believe that these two objects represented the normal state of affairs, and that the empire shown on the map and the heroic example of its servants were immutable facts, not subject to change. I sometimes wonder what my old headmaster would make of the United Nations, and the changes it has wrought on the map of the world.

When World War II ended forty-three years ago, 800 million people—just over a quarter of the world's population at that time—lived under colonial rule. Now less than 3 million people live under colonial rule in a world with a population twice as large as it was in 1945. The international community in the United Nations today numbers 159 states. The great competing empires are a thing of the past.

The American contribution to this basic change in the political setup on our planet was decisive. The idea that after a great world war none of the victors should gain any new territory—in itself a revolutionary idea—emerged during World War I under the inspiration of President Woodrow Wilson. The idea that empires as such are not a good thing is also very American. The basic principle underlying this remarkable change in the way we look at the world was the concept of self-determination. This concept surfaced in the eighteenth century, began to take practical form with the American Revolution, and gradually evolved as a concomitant of the emerging nationalism of the nineteenth century.

Self-determination became an important principle on the international stage at the end of World War I. Woodrow Wilson enunciated this principle when he told the Congress in 1919: "Every people should be left free to determine its own polity."[2] In Wilson's Fourteen Points, self-determination is not specifically mentioned, but the autonomous development of the territories of the German, Austro-Hungarian, and Turkish empires is an important theme of the Points.

After World War I the implementation of the principle of self-determination did not lead to very stable conditions or have uniformly happy results. The dissolution of the Turkish and Austro-Hungarian Empires spawned a host of troubles, some of which are still with us. Namibia, for example, and the problem of Palestine originated in the arrangements made at the end of World War I. Hitler even managed to invoke the principle of self-determination in order to justify taking over Czechoslovakia. Demonstrating how easily a noble concept can be twisted, he said: "In 1918, Central Europe was torn up and reshaped by some foolish or crazy so-called statesmen under the slogan 'self-determination and the right of nations.' . . . To this, Czechoslovakia owed its existence. . . . at last, nearly twenty years after, Mr. Wilson's right of self-determination for the 3,500,000 [Germans in Czechoslovakia] must be enforced and we [that is, Nazi Germany] shall not just look on any longer."[3] This highly cynical remark illustrates the perennial problem of the practical meaning of self-determination.

By the end of World War II, the concept of self-determination had taken on a wider meaning. Once again, there was to be no territorial aggrandizement for the victors in the war. But the principle of self-determination was now to be applied not just to the imperial possessions of enemies which had been vanquished in war, but, much to the distress of some of my British compatriots and other European colonial powers, to *all* colonial empires. Self-determination had become the right of all peoples to choose their own form of government. The idea, as evolved in President Roosevelt's Washington during the discussions of the early drafts of the United Nations Charter, was to bring colonial territories to independence in an *orderly* way. This was a much more sweeping concept than anything that Woodrow Wilson had in mind, for the United States was now maintaining that decolonization was a logical extension of the aims for which the Allies had fought the war.

Ralph Bunche was an important and active participant in the United States team which drafted the chapter of the United Nations Charter on decolonization and trusteeship. In a speech in 1946 he said that the treatment of non-self-governing peoples "involves a searching test of the ability of the postwar world to give effect to the ideals and principles for which World War II was fought to its victorious conclusion."[4] Although the European colonial powers, and not least Winston Churchill, were not exactly overjoyed at the implications of this policy, the United States prevailed. There was still, however, little realistic grasp of exactly how the decolonization process would work and what the timing was to be. It was generally thought that decolonization might, with luck, be completed in about a hundred years. Nor was it quite clear how it was going to happen in practice. Wendell Willkie, for example, in 1942, had referred to the "orderly but scheduled abolition of the colonial system."[5] What did that really mean?

Self-determination involved two main problems: To whom did the principle of self-determination apply, and by what process was independence from colonial rule to be realized? The principle was certainly going to be applied to all colonies, or non-self-governing territories as they were called in the Charter, but other questions remained. Did it, for example, apply to the Palestinians? As we are reminded every day, this remains a violently controversial question. Was it to apply to very large groups within independent countries who had ethnic and other reasons to claim autonomy, or even self-government—as in Nigeria, for example, or East Pakistan, or Katanga, the richest province of the Belgian Congo—or Scotland, or Wales, or Northern Ireland for that matter? How small a group could qualify for self-determination and nationhood? The problem of mini-states is an interesting subject that I shall not attempt to discuss here.

After the decolonization process was well advanced and the Third World majority began to take hold, these questions led to some rather curious decisions in the United Nations. In general it was agreed that no subsequent action could disrupt the unity, independence, and territorial integrity of a country that had gained its independence from its former colonial status. Many African boundaries imposed in the European colonial race of the late nineteenth century do not make much sense economically or ethnically, some of them even being simply along lines of longitude and latitude. But the African states decided that if they were to give up these boundaries, it would be completely impossible to determine new boundaries. Thus, the Organization of African Unity has insisted that the boundaries which existed at independence must be maintained.

There are other problems. If independence means the majority choosing how it wants to be governed, what about British colonies like Gibraltar or the Falklands, in which a majority population favors remaining a British colony? What about Hong Kong, which, for larger political reasons, the British have decided, in the context of their new relationship with China, to leave—something that many of the inhabitants didn't want at all? What about the Soviet republics, or the former Baltic states? Does self-determination apply to them? Evidently, some peoples are more self-determinant than others—not a very satisfactory conclusion.

The second problem was how this rather inexact concept was going to be realized. The United States originally preferred a peaceful transition, preferably through an intermediate phase of trusteeship, during which the colonial peoples would be able to develop self-governing institutions. During this period the colonial powers would be answerable to the General Assembly of the United Nations, where the United States at that time enjoyed an unchallenged majority. One of the many ironies of decolonization is that, by insisting on the decolonization process, the United States destroyed that majority, and its own enthusiasm for the General Assembly waned accordingly.

The moment the process of decolonization started, with the independence of India in 1947, any idea of an orderly timetable or a controlled process became unrealistic. The avalanche of decolonization developed a momentum of its own. In just two decades ninety-four new states were created, eighteen of them in 1960 alone. Any idea of the leisurely and "scheduled" progress to independence, or the interim phase of trusteeship, also vanished. It is a fact that if human beings are offered a choice between freedom to make their own mistakes and security as a colonial territory, they will usually choose freedom and independence, no matter where it may take them. There can be no denying that, up to now, the results of the decolonization process have been uneven, but that fact in no way impugns the validity of the right to independence.

Our prosperous, industrialized society has sometimes expressed exasperation with the countries of the Third World. It is therefore important to remember that because of their colonial status a majority of the newly independent countries missed the greatest economic boom in history—the Industrial Revolution. Most of them had no role in it at all, except as a source of raw materials and primary products. Thus, when independence cast them into the highly competitive world of independent sovereign states, the developing countries were nearly two hundred years behind. The early radicalism and rhetoric of Third World countries in the United Nations was to a large extent a reflection of this historical disadvantage. Ralph Bunche made a prophetic statement about this phenomenon in 1946: "The needs and expectations of all of us in these strenuous days of modern times are great enough, to be sure, but the needs and the expectations of non-self-governing peoples are greater. The reason is simple: They start with less and therefore they both need and aspire to more."[6]

Keen as they were on the principle of self-determination, the founding fathers of the United Nations seem to have shown less interest in its practical consequences. The main thrust of the United Nations in the immediate postwar years was for collective security, disarmament, and postwar reconstruction. The transformation of the colonial system and its gradual liquidation took a secondary place in the postwar scheme of things, and its implications for the development of the United Nations were not clearly analyzed or foreseen.

We can now see that there was already emerging a new international constituency representing the majority of the human race. This constituency had very different interests from the governments that wrote the UN Charter and set the organization up. It was primarily interested in economic development and, of course, the completion of the decolonization process.

In their first years in the United Nations, the newly independent countries engaged in a great deal of radical rhetoric, insisting, for example, on a plan for a New International Economic Order, which the old countries found not only unrealistic but insulting. There were other developments, such as the tilt against Israel, which has had a profound effect on the attitude of the West, and especially of the United States, to the world organization. The result was a loss of enthusiasm in Western countries for the international organization that they had originally sponsored. In the interests of all the member nations it is to be hoped that we are now seeing the beginning of a reversal of this trend.

While the new international constituency, later called the Third World, was emerging, the capacity of the United Nations to maintain international peace and security was largely paralyzed by the antagonism of its two most powerful members, the Soviet Union and the United States. There was thus little to prevent difficulties between the new nations from leading to open conflict.

In the first phase of decolonization, a number of power vacuums that occurred in the wake of decolonization were more or less successfully filled by international action. This did not mean that the United Nations solved the problems, but that it contained their potential for escalation. This was true initially in Palestine, Kashmir, Cyprus, and the Congo. Since, in the absence of East-West cooperation, it was impossible to deal with situations like this in the way that the Charter had intended, various new techniques evolved, including peacekeeping and the enhanced role of the Secretary-General. These conflict-control mechanisms prevented regional conflicts—some of them in extremely sensitive areas of the world—from becoming battlegrounds between East and West. This was a considerable achievement, if not a complete success.

In the second stage of the decolonization process the United Nations has been less successful, and in a number of cases, the superimposition of East-West rivalry has exacerbated regional conflicts. There have been many wars and conflicts since 1945. All have been fought with conventional weapons—not with the nuclear weapons which so preoccupy us—and most of them have been fought in the Third World with weapons provided by the First and Second Worlds. There have been tremendous casualties and destruction, not to mention the economic stress caused by developing countries seeking to acquire weapons systems they cannot afford. Some of these conflicts have also threatened to involve the nuclear superpowers.

A bitter Third World view of this phenomenon is emerging, as expressed in the following observation:

> This paradox of massive political and military investment (the latter largely in the form of arms transfers and military advisers) in insecure regimes on the part of the superpowers, which nevertheless stop short of a final commitment to save them when the chips are down, adds substantially to the problems of insecurity that many Third World regimes face; for it makes these regimes more reckless, more

repressive and less flexible on the mistaken notion that they will be bailed out by their superpower patrons when in dire straits.[7]

It is certainly true that until recently the nuclear superpowers have tended to be more concerned with their own mutual relationship than with the resolution of regional conflicts, or indeed with their Charter responsibility for maintaining peace and making the UN Security Council work. The tendency to take a Cold War view of regional conflicts has had lamentable consequences for the people directly concerned.

The past year has seen a welcome change in this pattern. It now seems possible that the United States and the Soviet Union can agree that at least some conflicts—for example, the war between Iran and Iraq—are simply too dangerous for them *not* to cooperate on. This is an important step. The next step will be to develop the international authority and the capacity for benevolent pressure to give reality to the decisions of the United Nations Security Council.

The lesson is the same as it was at the birth of the United Nations forty-three years ago. If we are to cope with the real problems of the future—not simply conflict situations from the past but the major problems which the whole human race will be facing in the next hundred years—we must renew our interest in evolving reliable and effective international systems.

The hard-won lesson of both world wars was that competing national security systems or military alliances lead to an arms race, which in turn leads to a situation where even a relatively small international misunderstanding or dispute in a sensitive area can trigger a major war. That was the reason why the founders of the United Nations were so anxious to establish a system of collective security. Supervised by the most powerful countries, this system would make it possible to scale down national security systems and thereby to achieve disarmament, or at least arms control, and therefore a far greater degree of stability and security in the world.

This seemed eminently sensible in 1945, after six years of world war. Now, however, such an idea is often regarded as naïve or even subversive. Will it take another world disaster to reinforce the lessons we have already learned in two world wars? If so, the outlook is grim, for we have created the weapons for a terminal disaster. We cannot afford another world war to convince us of what we know already. There is only one serious alternative—to make international institutions work properly.

The East-West problem or Cold War is now apparently more or less under control. But surrounding it in the Third World lies much volatile and explosive material. A misunderstanding or an unexpected chain of events in the Third World has always been the most obvious trigger for a fatal confrontation between the nuclear powers. In fact, this has come dangerously close to happening several times since 1945—in the Middle East, Africa, Asia, or over the Soviet missiles in Cuba.

Although the situation is more promising at the nuclear superpower level, nuclear proliferation and the reintroduction of chemical weapons in regional conflicts are ominous signals for the future. In the context of desperate political, social, or fundamentalist movements, fueled by despair, frustration, and poverty on a vast scale, this kind of threat to world peace cannot be ignored. Now less than ever can we afford to be ambivalent about making the international system for peace and security work.

It is high time for the great nations of the world to lead the way back to the system that was supposed to "save succeeding generations from the scourge of war."[8] General Secretary Gorbachev, in a surprising reappraisal of Soviet international policy that includes a reversal of many long-standing Soviet positions on international cooperation, has written:

> Why are we so persistent in raising the question of a comprehensive system of international peace and security? Simply because it is impossible to put up with the situation in which the world has found itself on the threshhold of the third millennium: In the face of the threat of annihilation, in a state of constant tension, in an atmosphere of suspicion and strife, spending huge funds and quantities of work and talent of millions of people, only to increase mutual mistrust and fears.[9]

Whatever Soviet intentions or motivations may be, the new Soviet approach has opened up new prospects for international cooperation. Gorbachev is saying very much what the West has been urging the Soviets to say for over forty years. There are many situations in the world where the new Soviet attitude can be tested. It has, for example, always been unlikely that the international community would be able to make serious progress on the problems of southern Africa *without* cooperation between East and West. Recent progress on the problems of Angola and Namibia are an example, among other things, of the effect of the new Soviet approach to regional conflicts.

Now that the nuclear superpowers are seemingly on the way to a more reliable system of avoiding a war between themselves, it should be possible for the United Nations to focus more effectively on the problem of conflict resolution in the Third World. The system devised forty-three years ago in the Charter was intended to provide the kind of assurance, benevolent pressure, and security which alone can produce the conditions for stability and peace. The conditions for making it more effective are now better than at any time in the history of the United Nations. Indeed the new climate is already beginning to show results. The test will be whether governments are prepared to take their security problems to the United Nations instead of going it alone in unilateral ventures that all too often end in disaster.

There are many other aspects of the results of decolonization which need to be addressed. One of the ironies of decolonization is that, despite gaining independence, the destinies of a great number of the former colonies are still shaped by outside forces. The turbulence of international markets has a devastating effect on the fragile economies of developing countries. All sorts of outside phenomena—high oil prices, fluctuations in commodity prices, exchange rate instability, the burden of debt—make the future of many of these countries doubtful and depressing. In the wasteland of burgeoning population, poverty, and despair, other powerful forces, fundamentalism and political radicalism, are taking root. If we are preoccupied, as we must be, by the necessity for a more stable world order, we have to make a dynamic effort not only to develop international means to keep the peace, but also to deal with the fundamental causes of social, economic, and political instability.

An international consensus for dealing with major conflicts in the Third World—in the Middle East, southern Africa, Central America, and Southeast Asia—now seems to be emerging. This is certainly a step forward, but these conflicts that grab the headlines should not remain the priority agenda of the next fifty years. The real agenda for the next generation is the series of irreversible changes that are now occurring in our relationship with the bountiful natural environment that we have always taken for granted. Questions of regional conflict, important though they are, should no longer be allowed to obscure that agenda.

Over the past forty years, great revolutionary forces have been set in motion—the surge of population, the demise of the family and of religion as stabilizing social forces all over the world, the move from the land to the cities, the rising tide of the destitute and the rejected in virtually all parts of the world, and the computerization that allows virtually instantaneous exchanges of information—including ebbs and flows of vast notional sums of money. We are witnessing the squandering of irreplaceable natural resources, massive assaults on the fragile ecosystem that has served us so well for so long—the upsetting of the balance of nature that has kept things going on this planet since the dawn of time. These are the real challenges of the future. We must learn to manage the conflicts we have inherited from the past, on which we now spend so much of our time and treasure, without any longer being dominated by them.

There are some promising signs. A more productive East-West dialogue is one of these. In the Third World itself, the rhetoric of the 1970s has given way to a less ideological, more pragmatic, constructive mood. One of the most significant developments of recent years has been the worldwide demise of Marxist economics. In the Third World there is a new generation of governments with little interest in ideology but extremely aware that their future depends on a more stable international system, in which they will play a respected role. This is a welcome challenge to leadership and to political creativity.

In the international arena, new ideas and institutions have usually emerged in response to terrible disasters. We can no longer afford this fatal form of stimulus. We must therefore try to make the giant step forward toward a workable international system simply because we know that the world we have created demands it. Such a step forward would be comparable on the international level to the transition that the more fortunate nations made, not so very long ago, to the nonviolent rule of law under representative government. If we give up this effort, our children and grandchildren will live, at best, in a steadily deteriorating environment and, at worst, in the shadow of imminent catastrophe.

In the last forty-five years we have revolutionized our world in many ways. For all its ups and downs, decolonization has given us, for the first time, the possibility of a world of independent sovereign states instead of an armed camp of antagonistic and acquisitive empires. This essential step toward a world of justice and liberty should provide the political base for more effective international institutions. We are only at the beginning. Determined work and imaginative leadership will be required if we are to achieve the international system that is demanded by the harsh realities of our time.

We have, as Dag Hammarskjold once said, created one world before we were ready for it. Our most urgent priority is to find a means of effectively managing that revolution.

2. The Question of Palestine

Perhaps the most complex and unique of all former colonial issues is the question of Palestine. This problem continues to assume new dimensions and to defy all efforts at settlement. It entails deep suffering and frustration on all sides, as well as a great waste of scarce resources. The Palestine problem is also of unique international importance. Not only does it constitute an ever-present threat to the wider peace, but the international community has assumed obligations to the peoples concerned that are perhaps more extensive and complex than its commitments to any other peoples in the world.

The basic issue is relatively simple. As the authors of the Peel report wrote in 1937, "No other problem of our time is so deeply rooted in the past."[1] The vivid language of the Old Testament reminds us that it is a problem of two ancient peoples in competition for a small, infinitely significant and precious homeland.

Here is a great historical tragedy which is also a threat to world peace. The path of violence, which is probably, in the short run, the easiest option for both sides, will certainly lead to disaster for both.

Each side has, or believes it has, an impeccable case. There is no likelihood of either giving up. They must, therefore, find a way to live together in peace. The question is how.

The year 1987 marked several significant anniversaries for the Palestine question. It was the ninetieth anniversary of Theodore Herzl's first Zionist World Congress; the seventieth anniversary of the Balfour Declaration, decreeing a Jewish homeland in Palestine; the fiftieth anniversary of the Peel report, suggesting separate Arab and Jewish states in Palestine; the fortieth anniversary of the United Nations Partition Plan which formalized that idea; the twentieth anniversary of the Six-Day War and Resolution 242, which, calling as it does for the security of all states within agreed borders and the return of occupied territories in exchange for peace, remains the only accepted basis for negotiation; the tenth anniversary of Anwar Sadat's dramatic voyage to Jerusalem; and the fifth anniversary of the Israeli invasion of Lebanon. This year, 1988, marks the fortieth anniversary of Israeli statehood. These anniversaries afford a mere glimpse of the tangled skein of events and ideas that make up the problem of Palestine.

Before World War I, there was no Palestine problem as such. Palestine was part of the Ottoman Empire, and its population was 90 percent Arab. After the defeat of the Turks by the British in the First World War and the collapse of the Turkish Empire, the present dimensions of the problem began inexorably to develop.

The contradictory promises made by the British in pursuit of their own war objectives bedeviled

the question from the start. To encourage the re-
volt against Turkey, they had promised the Arabs
independence in the former Turkish area that the
Arabs had been led to believe included Palestine.
To win world Jewish support in their war with the
Central Powers, the British, in the Balfour Declaration of 1917, promised a "national home for the
Jewish people" in Palestine, adding that this should
take place without prejudicing the rights of "exist-
ing non-Jewish communities of Palestine."[2] At
the 1919 peace conference, the Arabs had their
first taste of disappointment and disillusionment.
Palestine was to be under international administration, and in 1920 the Palestine Mandate was
allotted to Britain. Unlike other League of Nations mandates, there was no provision for termi-
nation and only a very vague reference to self-
determination. Although the text of the Balfour
Declaration was included in the mandate agreement, Trans-Jordan was excluded from the scope
of the Balfour Declaration for purposes of carrying
out the Palestine Mandate.

In spite of this inauspicious start, the early years
of the Palestine Mandate were relatively quiet,
but the gulf between the Arab and Jewish communities in Palestine was already fixed and steadily
widened. Then in 1933 Adolf Hitler came to power
in Germany. The Jews had constituted 8 percent of
the total Palestine population in 1917, but by 1939
there were 450,000 Jews in Palestine, or 30 percent
of the population. Tensions inevitably grew. There
were various international commissions and stud-
ies, but none could resolve the contradiction between the Arab claim to self-government and the

Jewish claim to a national home. In 1937 the Peel Commission suggested for the first time that there should be two states in Palestine, and in 1939 the British White Paper also suggested a binational state and set a quota of 75,000 for Jewish migration over the next five years, after which the consent of the Arabs would be required for further immigration. With the Nazi holocaust of the Jews of Europe, the question of Jewish immigration became the basic issue, because it would eventually determine the nature of the future Palestinian state.

At the end of World War II, as the whole world was struggling to pull itself together again, the situation in Palestine steadily deteriorated. Various efforts were made to cope with the problem. There was an Anglo-American Commission in 1946, which again put forward the concept of a binational state. There was growing and violent resistance against the British mandatory authorities, particularly on the Jewish side, including an extraordinarily effective campaign of violence and terrorism by the Irgun Zvei Leumi, led by Menachem Begin, and the Stern Gang, in which Itzhak Shamir was intimately involved.

Britain became the target of virtually universal criticism and harassment for its stewardship in Palestine. Britain was at that time undergoing a severe postwar economic crisis, and its desire and will to stay on as the mandatory power in Palestine steadily weakened. Britain brought the question to the United Nations, which, on the basis of a study by the Special Committee on Palestine, voted in 1947, by a narrow margin, for the partition plan setting up Arab and Jewish states in Palestine. The plan was rejected out of hand by the Arabs, and as the situation steadily deteriorated in Palestine, the British announced that they would withdraw on May 14, 1948.

In theory, the British were handing over the mandatory power to a UN administration. The day the British left, however, Israel declared its statehood and was immediately recognized by both the United States and the Soviet Union, followed by a number of other powers. Within that same twenty-four hours, on May 14 and 15, the new state of Israel was invaded by the armies of five Arab states. This war became the first challenge for the UN mediator, Count Folke Bernadotte, who was appointed by the General Assembly to search urgently for a settlement of the Palestine problem. Bernadotte contrived to get the war stopped for four weeks in June and then again in July—the first and second truces, which were supervised by UN observers. He himself was assassinated in Jerusalem on September 17 by the Stern Gang.

This, as it turned out, was virtually the end of the search for a comprehensive settlement of the Palestine problem as a first priority. Instead attention became concentrated on getting armistices between Israel and the Arab states and dealing with the burgeoning Palestine refugee problem. Ralph Bunche, who succeeded Bernadotte as mediator, managed to negotiate armistice agreements through a brilliant series of negotiations on the island of Rhodes and elsewhere. These agreements provided the basis for a supervised cessation of hostilities on the borders on the new state of Israel. The mediator's task was taken over by the UN Palestine Conciliation Commission, but the search for a permanent settlement was virtually abandoned.

In the succeeding years the armistice agreements were gradually eroded, particularly on the Israel-Syria front. At the same time, new elements emerged. One was the emergence of Arab nationalism, spearheaded by President Nasser of Egypt, a charismatic figure then (and indeed now) in the Arab world. The weight of the Arabs in the international community also increased with the development of their oil resources. A new and, to the West, unwelcome complication was the beginning of the involvement of the Soviet Union in Middle East affairs in the form of its close relations with, and provision of arms to, Egypt. These and other developments led, in 1956, to the Suez crisis, which once again distracted attention from the problem of the future of the Palestinians. We are reaping the fruits of that neglect today.

The Suez disaster, in which the United Kingdom and France connived with Israel, ostensibly to establish peace along the canal, but in fact to topple Nasser, which they failed to do, effectively destroyed the British and French influence, which had been until that time a dominant factor in the Middle East. The influence of the United States and the Soviet Union increased accordingly.

For ten years after Suez the United Nations Emergency Force (UNEF) kept the peace in Sinai and on the frontiers between Israel and Egypt, which had formerly been the most disorderly of all the Arab-Israeli frontiers. There was a wishful tendency among governments to believe that this was a permanent arrangement. As a result the core of the question, the future of the Palestinians themselves, continued to be ignored.

The UNEF arrangement collapsed in 1967, when Nasser demanded the withdrawal of UNEF from Egyptian soil. He was legally entitled to do this because UNEF's presence on Egyptian territory was subject to Egyptian sovereign agreement, and Nasser had always made it clear that, as a sovereign right, he could ask for its withdrawal. It was of no avail to point out to Nasser, as UN Secretary-General U Thant and others did, that this was going to precipitate a major disaster for the Arab states, for Israel was bound to respond with force to Nasser's closing of the Straits of Tiran, the access to the southern Israeli port of Eilath.

Nasser had a perfect right to plunge over the cliff, and he did. This was a historic miscalculation, which at one fell swoop lost to the Arab countries Sinai, Jerusalem, the West Bank, Gaza, and the Golan Heights in Syria. Thus was added to an already complicated situation a terrible new dimension, the problem of the Israeli-occupied territories, which greatly increased the number of Palestinians under Israeli occupation. Out of this disaster in November 1967 came Security Council Resolution 242, which was considered at the time to be a great diplomatic triumph—a triumph claimed, incidentally, by quite a wide range of authors. The resolution, which remains the only generally agreed basis for a settlement of the Arab-Israel problem, calls for the security of all states in the region, including Israel, within agreed borders, and the return of territories occupied by Israel. It does *not* specifically deal with the question of the future of the Palestinians. In retrospect, it is easy to see that this has been a fatal flaw in the perception of the Palestine problem ever since 1948.

From the early 1960s a new generation of Palestinians, frustrated and embittered by international promises that never came to anything practical, although they were reasserted every year in resolutions of the UN General Assembly, took increasingly to violence. The Palestine Liberation Organization came into being, and a steady crescendo of terrorism began to put the Palestinian question on the world map again—aircraft highjacking, assassinations, attacks on civilians, and so on.

Frustration was also rising in another quarter. The new president of Egypt, Anwar Sadat, may have appeared less belligerent and intransigent than Nasser. In retrospect he also appears to have been more practical. Sadat made a series of gestures to prove that he wished to achieve the withdrawal of the Israelis from Sinai peacefully. He accepted the proposal of the UN special representative, Ambassador Gunnar Jarring, for the exchange of occupied territory for peace with Israel, something that no Arab leader had done before. He initiated a determined effort in the UN Security Council, which unfortunately nobody except Egypt took seriously.

These peaceful overtures found no response. As a result, in October 1973, Sadat undertook something that Israel did not believe he was capable of doing, a frontal assault across the Suez Canal into Israel-occupied Sinai. This provided, among other things, a remarkable example of the fallibility of large intelligence organizations. Neither Israeli intelligence nor the United States CIA took Egyptian preparations along the canal seriously, apparently because they did not believe that the Egyptians were capable of crossing the canal, or even of thinking of such a thing.

The 1973 war created a new atmosphere. It engendered a more pragmatic mood in Israel and, on Sadat's side, a new willingness to go to the negotiating table. The brilliant diplomacy of Henry Kissinger, as well as an imaginative use of the Security Council and the UN's peacekeeping capacity, put a stop to the fighting. The mounting of a Middle East Peace Conference under joint United States–Soviet auspices led to disengagement agreements, both on the Suez Canal and in the Golan Heights of Syria, negotiated by Kissinger and supervised by UN peacekeeping forces (UNEF II and United Nations Disengagement Observer Force [UNDOF]). For several years the Middle East Peace Conference was regarded as the best hope for a more general settlement, but the inability of the parties to agree as to who was to represent the Palestinians made it impossible to reconvene it.

Sadat finally grew impatient with efforts to resummon the Middle East Peace Conference and, to virtually universal surprise, flew to Jerusalem in November 1977. This led to the American-sponsored Camp David negotiations, to the Israel-Egyptian Peace Treaty, and to the Camp David Accords, which were supposed to open the way to negotiation of the Palestinian problem on the basis of a preliminary period of autonomy leading to the negotiation of a final settlement.

The achievements of Camp David were violently resented by the Arab states, which believed that Egypt, by making a separate peace, had destroyed the unity of the Arab world which they believed to be the only way of getting a serious settlement with Israel. The "autonomy talks" never got going and, after the Egypt-Israel peace had been concluded with the withdrawal of Israel from Sinai, the Camp David process petered out. Once again there was no progress on the basic problem of the future of the Palestinians. On the Palestinian side this led to renewed bitterness and violence as well as to largely counterproductive rhetorical efforts in the United Nations and elsewhere.

On the Israeli side there was a radical change. With the arrival of Menachem Begin as prime minister in June 1977, the previous Israeli policy that Israel would, in the right circumstances, give up at least a substantial part of the occupied territories in return for peace began to give way to the doctrine of Eretz Israel, in which Judea and Samaria as a part of biblical Israel are an inalienable part of Israel itself. This was the basis on which, already in 1947, Begin had strongly opposed the UN partition plan.

The Israeli invasions of Lebanon in 1978 and 1982 and the destruction in 1982 of the PLO's power base in Beirut once again tended to distract attention from the Palestinian problem. No major negotiating initiatives were undertaken in the 1980s, and since November 1987, Palestinian bit-

terness and frustration have overflowed in an indigenous, widespread, grassroots rebellion, the In-
tifada, in the occupied territories of Gaza and the
West Bank. In mid-1988 King Hussein of Jordan
renounced his responsibility for the Palestinian
population of the West Bank and his authority to
negotiate on their behalf, thus removing the so-
called "Jordanian option," much favored in Israel
and the United States, from the negotiating table.

In December 1988, after a speech and press conference by Yasir Arafat in Geneva, in which he
gave assurances as to the recognition of the existence of Israel and the renunciation of terrorism,
the United States agreed to enter into talks with
the Palestine Liberation Organization. This decision was not welcomed by the new coalition
government of Prime Minister Shamir, who pro-
claimed that Israel would never negotiate with
the PLO. The future of negotiations for a settlement therefore remains obscure at the time of
writing.

What do we learn from this tragic history? First
that ancient roots, such as exist for both sides in
Palestine, are of tremendous importance and that
love of country is a predominant and basic moti-
vation on both sides. In a recent interview with an
Israeli lawyer, a journalist asked, "Why do you say
that deportation of Palestinians is a worse punish-
ment than imprisonment?" The Israeli lawyer an-
swered, "You don't understand the Palestinians.
For them, love of country is an overmastering emo-
tion, and therefore to be deprived of their home-

land is infinitely worse than to be imprisoned in it." He was right, and, if we forget that basic fact, we're not going to get anywhere.

The second lesson is that it serves little purpose to try to establish right and wrong, or which side has the best case. This is a great historical tragedy of two ancient peoples, two diasporas—one nearly two thousand years old and one much more recent—and one homeland. Incidentally, if further proof were needed, it is also an example of the deplorable results of imperial expediency. At the critical historical moment, the British saw Palestine more as a factor in imperial policy than as an important problem in itself. There is a more contemporary lesson of a similar kind: in our time it is essential that the Middle East question should not be viewed primarily as a factor in the Cold War. This approach is likely to be disastrous not only for the Israelis and the Arabs, but also for the powers of East and West. The current trend toward American-Soviet cooperation in the resolution of regional conflicts is welcome—and long overdue. It has yet to be applied to the Israel-Palestinian-Arab problem.

The final lesson is that unanticipated historical factors are likely to overturn even the best laid plans. Hitler was not foreseen when the Balfour Declaration was promulgated in 1917, nor was the emergence of the wealth and power of the Arabs due to oil. We would be wise to wonder what unanticipated factors may appear in the future. The possibilities include the spread of fundamentalism in that part of the world, the ever-present danger of nuclear proliferation, the reintroduction of chemical warfare and the possibilities of long-range missile warfare.

The international importance and urgency of peace and a settlement in the Middle East, or in what used to be called Palestine, is very great. We have already witnessed the makings of a major East-West confrontation in the Suez Crisis of 1956 and again in 1973, when what had started as a joint US-Soviet effort to end the war became, for two or three days, a major potential confrontation between the nuclear superpowers.

The Palestine issue is not just a terribly difficult regional problem; it is a major factor in the peace of the world. It represents a challenge to international organizations, especially the United Nations. Palestine was the first great practical challenge to the authority of the United Nations, and the events of 1948 showed that this authority could not be exercised in the way that up to that point people had believed it could: namely, by the unanimous exercise of influence, and, if necessary, military force by the great powers of the world. Even though the great powers in the Security Council had agreed on the substance of the question, they could not agree to enforce their decision. In fact, this negative experience gave birth to the technique called "peacekeeping," a nonviolent form of international conflict-control based on consent and voluntary cooperation rather than on force. Peacekeeping originated in the Palestine problem and developed there.

Another truth that emerges very clearly from this long, sad history is the importance of the negotiating process. Even when it doesn't appear to be going anywhere, the existence of an active negotiating process as a symbol of the care and concern of the world community is an extremely important element in maintaining stability and in strengthening and encouraging the moderates on all sides, without whom no solution will ever be achieved.

One of the great problems of the Palestine question has been that the antagonists have almost never been prepared to make the necessary concessions at the same time. It has happened over and over again. The partition plan was rejected by the Arabs, when no one except King Abdullah of Jordan saw clearly that it would have brought the Arabs closer to what they wanted than they have come at any subsequent time. Now, forty years later, the PLO is claiming the partition plan as the basis of a settlement. The Arab rejection, after the 1967 war, of Israel's offer to withdraw from all the occupied territories in exchange for peace passed up an opportunity that is unlikely to come again. With all the sympathy and understanding that the tragic plight of the Palestinians entitles them to, this self-defeating tendency must also be taken into account.

Unwillingness to compromise and make necessary concessions is now a problem on both sides. Indeed, it seems likely that if a settlement is to come, it will have to be pressed firmly on both sides by the international community. Liberation movements in exile have to believe that they have a justifiable maximum claim and that this claim can and must be recognized by everybody else.

For the Israelis, security considerations are paramount, and not only on account of recent Jewish history. Israel, even cushioned by the occupied territories, is a very small and vulnerable country, and security is therefore a basic preoccupation. This means that progress will demand not only benevolent pressure from outside, but also valid guarantees for all parties. The political leaders on all sides are not going to be able to make the concessions they will have to make in order to move toward a peaceful settlement without help, support, and stimulus from the outside.

Extreme partisanship for one side or the other in the outside world has often been the bane of international efforts to approach the Palestine problem. It projects the problem on to a much wider level without doing anything to help to solve it. With the recent example of US-Soviet cooperation in facing regional conflicts, it is to be hoped that this problem too may be overcome. A benevolent, impartial consensus in the world community could do much to persuade all the parties concerned to engage in constructive negotiations.

There are other parties to the dispute that have to be brought along. Recently King Hussein of Jordan formally relinquished to the PLO the representation of and responsibility for the Palestinians of the West Bank. This development underlines the necessity of the PLO, Israel, and the United States making the moves necessary to allow a serious discussion of the future of the Palestinians and the occupied territories. Only in December 1988 did the PLO leadership finally make the public commitments on recognizing Israel and renouncing terrorism that allowed the United States to deal directly with it, while the Israeli leadership has recently repeated its vow never to deal with the PLO under any circumstances.

Syria must also somehow be brought along. It used to be said that you can't have a war in the Middle East without Egypt, and you can't have peace without Syria. The cooperation of the Soviet Union is particularly important in this connection. Meanwhile the uprising in the occupied territories continues. A serious framework for representative negotiation has never been more needed. If an international conference cannot be agreed upon, it would be well to consider the UN Security Council, now enjoying an unprecedented degree of unanimity, as a possible framework for negotiations. The council is, incidentally, the only forum where Israel and the PLO habitually sit at the same table as parties to a dispute.

What can be the shape of a possible agreement? A settlement must encompass Israeli security, an acceptable future for the Palestinians, the question of borders and the status of Jerusalem, which may well prove in the end to be the greatest problem of all. This is a very tall order. Quite apart from the seriousness of the present disorders, Israel is sitting on a demographic time bomb. If the present *status quo* persists, Israelis are likely, in the foreseeable future, to become a minority in their own country. This would create pressure for a repressive minority government which would be against the traditions and ideals of Israel. The Palestinians, for their part, are at present facing the prospect of indefinite occupation, repression and the destruction of their national identity. In these circumstances both sides can only expect a continued cycle of violence and disruption. Indeed this may well seem to many on both sides to be, at least for the short term, the easiest option. In the long run, the consequences of a violent deadlock could be disastrous not only for Israelis and Palestinians, but for world peace.

For both sides the negotiating process is literally the only hope of escaping a disastrous future. So far, most of the discussion about this process has been concerned with procedure—whether there is to be an international conference or direct negotiations, and so on. But what about the substance? It seems essential to have in mind, with full appreciation of the strong feelings and inevitable resistance involved, some idea of what a workable future arrangement could be—a general target to be aimed at in the negotiations. This will not, initially at any rate, be a popular exercise with either side, to put it mildly, but without a target, negotiating from zero could become endless and meaningless bargaining. One such target plan has been outlined by a British Labour member of Parliament, Gerald Kaufman: the continuation of the State of Israel as a Jewish homeland, containing a properly enfranchised Arab minority; and a Palestinian entity, with proper and acceptable arrangements made for self-determination and in which Jews are free to live if they accept the new arrangements. The two parts will have, for practical reasons, to be linked in some form of economic union or confederation. It sounds deceptively simple, but if the international community could rally round a formula of this kind, at least the search for a settlement that all the parties so desperately need would have some focus.

A new and realistic negotiation will depend on the willingness of all sides to consider the concessions that a real settlement will inevitably demand. It seems likely that such a settlement can be reached only with a considerable degree of benevolent persuasion from the outside. It remains to be seen whether the world community is now capable of the degree of consensus and objectivity required to exert this persuasion effectively, and whether there is strong and imaginative enough leadership in Israel and on the Palestinian side to embark on negotiations and persist in them until the goal is reached. There is no shortage of ideas and proposals for a settlement. The international situation is now more favorable to such an effort than at any time since 1948, but the decision inevitably rests with the protagonists themselves. They alone can choose between some form of peaceful coexistence and a situation which is a deadly threat not only to the future of Palestinians and Israelis but also to international peace.

3. Decolonization in Africa: Experiences in International Responsibility

Looking back on the history of Africa for the last hundred or so years, one is inclined to question the applicability of the word "responsibility." European nineteenth-century colonialism in Africa, which has been the major force in recent African history, was rooted in the tremendous new power that European nations gained from two forces, industrialization and the new spirit of nationalism. The European powers were almost exclusively concerned with trade and with their rivalries with each other. For them the Africans seemed scarcely to exist at all as people, or so it must seem to us now. Their culture, their history, their society were almost totally ignored except by missionaries, and for all the European powers cared, they might never have existed. The Berlin Conference of 1884, which was called by the German emperor to consider various aspects of the future in Africa, was exclusively European and reflects purely European interests. There was no African representation at all. Although the subject was ostensibly the future of Africa, it was in fact much more the European balance of power.

The African colonies did not attract the attention of the colonial powers in the way that India or Indonesia or Indochina did. Except for an occasional drama like the Livingstone story or the dramatic defeat and death of General Gordon in Khartoum, Africa did not attract much attention, and at the governmental level it was perceived as lacking in economic and strategic importance. After World War I there was a certain reshuffling of African colonies to dispose of the former German territories, but from Africa only Ethiopia, Liberia, and the Union of South Africa were members of the League of Nations. Even after World War II, African decolonization seemed to be a distant prospect—something that nobody was really working very much to prepare for. Eventually it seemed to come as something of a surprise and an afterthought.

Tension soon arose between the old colonial powers, grimly trying to hang on, and the United States, where anticolonialism and enthusiasm for decolonization were expressed through the United Nations, an attitude referred to by one British official as "impractical doctrinaire idealism." There was a lot of this kind of snorting from the officials of the colonial powers. Nonetheless, after India gained its independence in 1947, the spirit of liberation was in the air. Arab nationalism was a rising force, and the wind of change began to blow around the world, although nobody realized quite how strong it was soon to become.

At the same time, decolonization began to play a role in the strategic and ideological concerns of the nuclear superpowers—the United States and the Soviet Union. As postcolonial power vacuums appeared in different parts of the world, and as Britain and France declined as world powers, the concerns of the Soviet Union and the United States became an important aspect of the decolonization process. The Suez Crisis in 1956 was a major turning point, dramatically marking the demise of the traditional British and French influence in the Mediterranean and the Middle East. That historic role vanished overnight, and as a result both the United States and the Soviet Union became increasingly concerned with the effects of decolonization in the Middle East itself, in Africa, and later on in Indochina. After being hailed in the days of postwar euphoria as the idealistic pursuit of a great goal of human justice, the decolonization process became increasingly confused with other aims and concerns.

In any circumstances the situation of the newly independent countries of Africa would have been difficult enough. Quite apart from world politics, world markets, and the strategic concerns of the major powers, they had to face a daunting series of practical domestic problems. Over the years, the original sponsors of decolonization, especially the United States, became increasingly discouraged by the performance of the newly independent countries which they had so ardently championed. Particularly disturbing was their failure to embrace, and stick to, democratic rule and to advance along the road of economic and social development which had been confidently assumed to be the natural path for them to follow.

The *aim* of decolonization is enshrined in Chapter 11 of the United Nations Charter. Unfortunately, the *method* by which it should be achieved was not enshrined in the Charter or anywhere else. This omission has nowhere been more important than in the experience of the African states.

What does decolonization actually mean, especially in Africa? Does it mean the transfer of power? Does it mean Africanization? Does it mean emancipation from European influence and control? Does it mean neocolonialism, by which Europeans will come back in another role and pull most of the strings? Does it mean a growing dependence on the international community? Or is it, in practice, a mixture of all those things?

The first African state to become independent was Libya, which was an exception to most of the rules and was not at all typical of the decolonization process. It was scarcely a state by any normal definition. It had been an Italian possession and consisted of three very different provinces. It was of strategic importance, because the British regarded it as their fallback base for the Middle East if they had to leave their Canal Zone bases in Egypt. Its future economic viability presented a considerable problem.

In the end the British, who had been toying with the idea of making a separate deal with King Idris of the Senussi, agreed instead to an arrangement whereby the United Nations decreed that Libya would become independent by the end of 1951. The British and the Libyans were fortunate that the United Nations appointed Adrian Pelt as the supervisor of the transition. Pelt did a remarkable

job of keeping the banner of international idealism aloft while at the same time making a number
of pragmatic deals for the benefit both of the Libyans and of the British, including the setting up of
military bases which, before its oil resources were
developed, provided Libya's only income.

Libya was not typical of the decolonization process. The Sudan, the largest territory in Africa and
one of the most important, became independent
in 1956, in the same year as Morocco and Tunisia.
The Sudan was also a state that was really not
one nation. The authority of the colonial power
had held together its northern and southern regions, which were ethnically and religiously completely different. Thus, when the Sudan became
independent, it faced—among other problems—a
great north-south dilemma that has not yet been
resolved.

The sudden and radical loss of world position
and power by France and Great Britain in 1956
echoed throughout the continent of Africa, along
with the perceived success of President Nasser,
the leader of Arab nationalism, in defying these
old colonial powers. This development did much
to set the tone for the extraordinary events of the
next five years, during which there was a veritable
landslide of independence in Africa. In 1957 Ghana
became independent under Kwame Nkrumah—
the model of the free-swinging liberation leader
who proved to be better at winning independence
than at administering it.

In 1958 the French avalanche began. General
DeGaulle, in his lofty way, had indicated that
French African territories should say yes or no to a

continued relationship with France. To his indignation and surprise, Sekou Touré of Guinea said no. This created a considerable stir and precipitated the liquidation of the French empire in Africa. It went very quickly, and by the end of 1960, with the exception of Algeria, all the French territories were independent.

The year 1960 was another turning point. This was the year in which the Congo and also Nigeria, the second largest country in Africa, became independent. The independence of the Congo precipitated new and disastrous problems as well as a major crisis in the United Nations itself. This was the point at which the problem of East-West rivalry began to impose itself like a dead hand on the already tumultuous situation in emergent Africa.

Apart from the colonial structure of the Belgian Congo, the vast territory—it is roughly the size of Western Europe—lacked the normal elements of a national state. Its ethnic diversity alone was of immense complexity, comprising more than two hundred tribal groups. The Congo's colonial boundaries were the main guarantee against its complete disintegration.

Another crucial factor was an almost total lack of preparation for independence. The first elections took place only in 1959, less than a year before independence, and only in January 1960, in a rather disorderly meeting in Brussels, was it decided that independence would take place at the end of June that same year. At that time only seventeen Congolese had university degrees. There were no Congolese officers in the Congolese army. Virtually none of the future Congolese ministers had had any experience of government or public administration.

The Belgians apparently assumed that after independence things would continue pretty much as before. The commander of the Belgian-officered army, the Force Publique, had caused to be written on blackboards in officers' messes throughout the Congo: "Après l'indépendence = Avant l'indépendence" ("After independence = Before independence"), meaning that after independence nothing would change. This was an extraordinary misperception of the psychology of independence.

Five days after independence the Congolese army mutinied against its Belgian officers. The Belgians panicked and left the country. The Belgian government then sent back Belgian paratroops, which caused the Congolese in their turn to panic. The general panic caused a total collapse of the elaborate colonial structure of logistics and administration. On top of that, one week into independence, the richest province, Katanga, seceded under Moise Tshombe, who declared an independent state of Katanga.

The personalities of the people in charge were an important element in the confusion. The president was Joseph Kasavubu, a rather taciturn and stolid man; the wild card was the prime minister, Patrice Lumumba, a nationalist demagogue. Like his colleagues, he had virtually no experience of government. The Western media soon began to refer to Lumumba as pro-Soviet, but it would be hard to imagine anyone less likely to be a Soviet puppet. He was an outstanding loose cannon. Conversations with Lumumba would go rapidly from one extreme, such as expelling the UN with considerable bloodshed, to the other, which was brotherly friendship and requests for help. They would usually end up somewhere in the middle. Liberation leaders like Lumumba are, understandably, ready to take help or money from any source. Lumumba was fundamentally a nationalist, and a very excitable one. Kasavubu and Lumumba appealed to the United Nations for military as well as civilian assistance in getting the Belgian army out and establishing their own administration.

From the start, a major problem for the UN in the Congo was the anxiety of both the United States and the Soviet Union about the strategic control of this important and rich country. The Soviet Union did not want to see the Congo fall completely under American domination, and the United States had no intention of allowing it to fall under Soviet domination. Thus, in addition to all the other problems of the Congo, something like a proxy war—a war of secret agencies, the KGB and the CIA—was soon going on for what was left of the hearts and minds of the Congolese. This was a disastrous complication. The original government split up after two months, the West backing Kasavubu and Joseph Mobutu, and the East backing Lumumba; Lumumba was murdered in early 1961; and after many vicissitudes Mobutu came to power, apparently for life. The country's territorial integrity within its original borders, for which the United Nations had striven for four arduous years, was maintained.

There were three major secessionist movements in the Congo—Katanga, Kasai, and Orientale—but the Congo wasn't balkanized, as it well might have been. The United Nations, which paid a very heavy cost for this achievement, including the loss of Dag Hammarskjold and a major constitutional crisis over peacekeeping, achieved its basic objectives in the face of extraordinary hazards and difficulties. The practical consequences of the US-Soviet rivalry were kept out of the Congo (now Zaire); its boundaries were preserved as they had been at independence; and through nearly four years of civil war the rudiments of government and administration were preserved and developed by the UN. Now Zaire has what one author has called "a regime of organised pillage."[1] It is also a regime of surprising stability and durability. Is this the best that could be expected for the second largest nation in Africa?

When in 1962, after a long and bitter war, Algeria at last became independent, the remaining African colonial problems were the Portuguese possessions and Rhodesia and Namibia. The Portuguese under President Salazar had tried to ignore the wind of change in Africa. They had been in Africa longer than any other colonial power, and they intended to stay there. It took fifteen years of guerrilla war, and then a revolution in Portugal itself, before Angola and Mozambique became independent in 1975. Even then their troubles were far from over. Partly due to the nature and length of the resistance struggle, both countries installed Marxist governments designed to be as unlike the colonial pattern of rule as possible. Whatever the practical merits of this objective, one result was to arouse the obsessive anticommunism of the Republic of South Africa. The history of Mozambique and Angola, from 1975 until 1988, is a history not only of questionably effective Marxist regimes, but also of the perennial effort by South Africa to destabilize these regimes by military incursions and military aid to opposition movements. For many years several thousand South African soldiers actually operated in southern Angola, and at various times they went further north, on one occasion nearly to Luanda, the capital.

The independence of the Portuguese colonies left only Rhodesia, a British territory which had declared, under a white minority government, its illegal and unrecognized independence, and Namibia, formerly German Southwest Africa, where South Africa had, in the teeth of international opposition, hung onto its League of Nations mandate and remained in control. Rhodesia was another turning point. Against the wishes of the white minority regime of Ian Smith, a British conservative government successfully negotiated the colony's independence under the name of Zimbabwe. This successful effort was carried out with the active and imaginative support of the African front-line states, and particularly of Marxist Mozambique's President, Samora Machel. The Zimbabwe settlement has turned out to be a remarkable success.

With Zimbabwe independent, the former colonial powers of Europe banded together with the United States to try to do something about Namibia. On the initiative of the Carter administration, the so-called Western Contact Group, comprising the Western members of the Security Council, in 1978 secured the passage of Security Council Resolution 435, which set out a plan for the independence of Namibia. In 1980 it appeared, after intensive negotiations, that the implementation of this plan might be in sight.

The Reagan administration adopted a new policy in relation to South Africa—"constructive engagement"—which halted the momentum that had been generated on the problem of Namibia. The presence of Cuban forces in Angola became the determining factor in the initiation of the Namibian independence plan. Little progress was made for more than seven years. In 1988, however, in the improved international climate caused by Gorbachev's revision of Soviet international policy and the new relationship between the United States and the Soviet Union, the United States–sponsored negotiations between Angola, South Africa, and Cuba began to make remarkable progress. South African forces left Angola in August 1988. In December 1988 an agreement was signed at the United Nations providing for the withdrawal of Cuban troops from Angola within two years and for the implementation of the independence plan for Namibia outlined in Security Council Resolution 435 of 1978, starting on April 1, 1989.

In the Introduction to *Decolonization and African Independence*, Roger Louis writes the following:

The African states at the time of independence inherited: international boundaries; military and police forces that could, with varying degrees of efficiency, hold the state together; a revenue system
based on agricultural products and raw materials,
the external value of which would fluctuate with
the world market; in the British and French cases,
either elected local legislatures or elected representatives in a metropolitan parliament; and, usually, a
network of government offices complete with files,
typewriters, and telephones. There were great dis-
crepancies in economic resources and size as well
as in training and competence of officials.[2]

In the event this was not as useful an inheritance for many of these states as was originally
hoped. The resurgence of the basic tribal patterns
of African society which had been submerged in
colonial arrangements, led, in some cases, to major
secessionist movements. New elites emerged that
were primarily concerned with personal gain and
prestige and that tended, insofar as they were for
anything except themselves, to be for the urban
population at the expense of the rural population.
Such trends were not foreseen by the idealists of
the late forties. The superimposition of East-West
rivalries on some African problems exacerbated
them even further. It is to be hoped that this period is now at an end.

The effects of outside commercial interests and
the whiplash effect of oscillations in the world
market can spell disaster for developing countries.
Not all the efforts by well-meaning people and
organizations to superimpose on African coun-

tries the aims and the values of the developed world have proved helpful or applicable to their problems, state of development, and lack of infrastructure. There have also been persistent natural disasters—drought, flood, and famine—and new tribulations such as the AIDS epidemic.

In early 1960, at the beginning of Africa's great year of independence, Dag Hammarskjold went on a tour of Africa. That wise and sensitive man drew a lot of conclusions that seem to be even more valid now than they were then. He said that Africa was the greatest challenge to the performance and the conscience of the international community and that, if that challenge was not met, the results would be disastrous. He was critical of the lack of vision being shown, especially in the West, about the true nature of this challenge. On his return he wrote, "Africa is a part of the world which at present is outside the conflict, the competition, the Cold War . . . under which we are all suffering at present, and I would like to see that part of the world remain outside."[3] Later in the same year he himself got caught in the East-West nutcracker in the Congo.

Hammarskjold's views are particularly relevant to the present situation in southern Africa. In southern Africa, apart from the general problems of development and management, there are two basic problems: the failure to bring about the independence of Namibia, and the problem of apartheid in South Africa itself. The tragic situation in Angola and Mozambique and South Africa's efforts to destabilize the other black African states bordering on South Africa were closely linked to these two basic problems.

The adoption of Marxist-style regimes in the former Portuguese colonies, as well as Soviet, Cuban, and East European support of those regimes, until recently provided South Africa with a pretext for claiming support in the United States for South Africa's alleged resistance to Soviet expansionism, which took the form of backing anti-government movements such as UNITA in Angola and RENAMO in Mozambique. This proved for some time to be a quite effective policy. The front-line states were kept destabilized, "freedom fighters" in Mozambique and Angola were supported and encouraged, and South Africa played effectively on the United States' fear of Soviet expansionism. For the people of Angola and Mozambique especially, this was catastrophic.

It now seems that the new Soviet policy of cooperation within the United Nations for the resolution of regional conflicts may be bearing its first fruits in southern Africa. This development may make possible at last the evolution of a long-term and comprehensive international policy in southern Africa that would take into account all the many interrelated parts of the situation—political, military, economic, and social—in the interests of all the peoples of the region.

A genuine international consensus for action in this region, and the possibility of joint United States–Soviet initiatives evidently have great significance for South Africa. The current developments and a strengthening of the front-line states, with their reasonable and pragmatic approach to problems, may well be key factors in providing the context for South Africa to rethink its approach to the deep-rooted problem of apartheid.

The inheritance of black Africa at independence was a difficult one to build on. The economic and practical implications of this inheritance were well described in the early 1960s by Sylvanus Olympio, the first president of Togo:

> By breaking up Africa into economic and commercial compartments the colonial powers did their greatest harm. The effect of their policy has been the economic isolation of peoples who live side by side, in some flagrant instances within a few miles of each other, while directing the flow of resources to the metropolitan countries. For example, although I can call Paris from my office telephone in Lomé, I cannot place a call to Lagos in West Africa only 250 miles away. Again, while it takes a short time to send an airmail letter to Paris, it takes several days for the same letter to reach Accra, a mere 120 miles away.
>
> Other problems are more serious. Trade is the most effective method of creating good will among nations, but in Africa trade barriers are legion. Railroads rarely connect at international boundaries, and where they do, differences in gauges necessitate trans-loading. Highways have been constructed from the coast inland, but very few connect at economic centers of trade. The productive central regions of Togo, Dahomey and Ghana are as remote from each other as if they were on separate continents. These are the problems which we must tackle first.[4]

A later comment on the present situation occurs in *Decolonization and African Independence:*

> . . . Africa possesses some of the least viable states in the world. These states are weakly integrated into the world market because they are endowed with so few resources worth exploiting. In the last decade, moreover, some of them have suffered ecological trauma in the form of drought and famine. Areas of Africa are victims of natural catastrophe as well as civil war. They suffer also from basic flaws in economic planning. . . . The golden dreams of independence have been shattered because tropical Africa has not been able to sustain rates of growth and patterns of development that might have enabled Africans at least to improve their condition, if not to close the gap with the affluent West.[5]

The list of Africa's problems is long and daunting—declining self-sufficiency, plunder by self-seeking elites, civil war, demoralization, recurrent natural disasters, AIDS. Sound nation-building will be a long and demanding task, and much international help will be required. There are, however, encouraging signs of African reinvigoration and rethinking of problems. To mention only one recent example, the Special Session of the UN General Assembly adopted, on June 1, 1986, a plan of action, the first part of which deals with national action by African governments. Its new emphasis on self-help and indigenous initiative calls on the natural pragmatism and common sense of Africans.

In the meantime the problems and tribulations of many new African states present a compelling obligation for the international communtiy. In spite of its difficult past, the African continent could still demonstrate the success of wise international action. It presents both a challenge and an opportunity.

4. The Iran-Iraq War and Its Bearing on the Future of International Order

At the end of the Second World War, the quest for a collective system of international peace and security was a top priority for all governments. In the intervening years, however, both the confidence and the interest of governments in this great objective have weakened. The Iran-Iraq War provides a contemporary test case of the present strength of the international system for the maintenance of peace.

Decolonization and its results have been a major factor in the postwar world. As of March 1988, there were some twenty-five wars going on in the world—all of them in the Third World, and all of them fought with weapons from the First and Second Worlds. Four-fifths of the casualties in these wars have been civilians, and the estimated toll so far in these twenty-five wars alone is over three million people. This is a serious indictment of our efforts to build a collective security system convincing enough for nations to entrust their future to it rather than going it alone in unilateral military adventures that often end in disaster.

The worst of the Third World wars and the greatest casualties have been in Asia and in Africa, where the main objective has been to try to create or consolidate viable sovereign states out of the wreckage of the old European colonial empires. In some places, this process appears to be more or less over. In others, there are second-generation or even third-generation wars, like the hostilities in Indochina. Some new countries have had civil wars raging within their territories virtually ever since they became independent, like Angola and Mozambique. The death toll in wars since 1945 is estimated at something over seventeen million.

Until recently the two biggest wars were in Afghanistan, where the Soviet forces are now pulling out under an agreement negotiated by the United Nations, and the war between Iran and Iraq, in which hostilities were ended by a cease-fire in August 1988. Neither of these conflicts was directly connected to decolonization, but in different ways they underline the complications of the international situation which has succeeded the era of colonialism and imperialism, the relationship of the two nuclear superpowers and its effect on world order, and the problems of keeping the peace in a world of more than 160 independent sovereign states.

What should be the nature of international authority and responsibility in such a world? Until 1939, actual international authority resided mostly in the power of great empires, and sometimes this was a stabilizing, even beneficial, influence. My compatriots somewhat smugly described their own period of imperial power as the Pax Britannica. The British have always been good at public relations. The Romans, with their Pax

Romana, were also good at putting their imperial arrangements in a positive light. When the political map of the world consisted mostly of empires, the rights of nations and international law—what there was of it—took second place to imperial power.

The United Nations was supposed to replace this haphazard imperial system with a new and participatory, representative system of international authority and security. As I mentioned in an earlier chapter, imperialism had already received a mortal blow after World War I with the introduction of the principle of self-determination, and by the end of World War II the age of imperialism was all but over. Under the United Nations Charter, the world was to consist of sovereign independent states whose relations were to be governed by reason and the peaceful settlement of disputes, not by the use of force. Decolonization was to be an important factor in bringing this new world into being.

In theory the UN system was going to take the place of the imperial system. In practice that hasn't proved quite so easy. The decolonization process created power vacuums in many parts of the world, which in turn gave rise to conflicts. At the same time the split between East and West—the Cold War—paralyzed the authority of the new system centered on the UN Security Council that was supposed to regulate conflict. The net result has been a divided world, a vast nuclear and conventional arms race, conflict and disarray in the Third World, and a growing disillusionment with the international structure—the United Nations—

that was set up to make the world a more orderly, peaceful, and just place.

The Iran-Iraq War provides a striking example of the present shortcomings of the international system for peace and security. Estimates of casualties in the Iran-Iraq War run between 400,000 and 800,000. Of the twenty-five wars I mentioned earlier, only Afghanistan, Ethiopia, and Mozambique are in that casualty class. The Gulf War was a serious, dangerous war by any standard, and almost every government in the world had an interest in seeing it stopped, preferably without either side actually winning.

At first sight, the Iran-Iraq War might seem to be precisely the kind of conflict the United Nations was set up to deal with. One country invaded another. Neither country was a particularly popular member of the international community, and neither had particularly strong ties to either East or West. Both were economically dependent on a single primary commodity, oil, and neither had an arms production capacity of its own. The war might therefore have been expected to be an opportunity to show that the collective security system of the Security Council of the United Nations could work as it was originally set up to work, by persuasion and the use, as necessary, of enforcement measures.

If we wish to understand the difficulties of establishing a system of world order, it is important to study the reasons why this didn't happen. Only a reasonable degree of international peace and order will allow governments to face up to the real challenges of the coming years, which are not so much residual conflicts from the past as the global problems which we have created and which must be faced together and soon if we are not going to bequeath a dismal future to our children. Significant work on such problems will also require a very considerable degree of effective international authority and respect for that authority. The current nature of international authority and the reasons for a striking failure to exercise it are therefore subjects of major importance for the future.

A brief summary of the course of the war is as follows. In September 1980 Iraq invaded Iran, apparently in the hope of neutralizing the Islamic revolutionary government of Iran, whose activities it regarded as a threat to Iraq's own security. This attempt proved to be ill-judged. The war settled into a bloody stalemate, and two years later Iran counterattacked and occupied quite large areas of Iraqi territory. After a time the war of attrition was resumed. At the end of 1986, Iran launched another massive assault on the city of Basra, the second most important city of Iraq, and it appeared, at one point, as if that offensive might succeed. In January 1987 the Secretary-General of the United Nations, who had been trying throughout the war to negotiate a cease-fire as a prelude to a settlement, called upon the five permanent members of the Security Council to confer on what could be done to bring an end to the war.

The resulting unanimous adoption of Security Council Resolution 598 on July 20, 1987, was a

notable achievement. By that time the war of attrition had been expanded to include the use of
long-range missiles on civilian targets and the use
of chemical warfare, both very dangerous portents
for the future. The tanker war in the Gulf, where
each side was trying to destroy the economic life-
line of the other, continued, despite the presence
of naval vessels from a number of nations including the United States and the Soviet Union. A
cease-fire finally came into effect in August 1988.
How was such a war permitted to go on for nearly
eight years?

Although a treaty on their differences had been
concluded by the two governments in Algiers in
1975, relations between Iran and Iraq had been
stormy for some time before the war. All through
1979 and 1980, after the Iranian Revolution, there
were incidents, accusations, and provocations of
one sort or another from both sides. In April 1980
an effort to assassinate Tariq Aziz, the deputy
prime minister of Iraq, by an Iraqi of Iranian ex-
traction was interpreted by the Iraqi government
as an officially sponsored attempt. There were
expulsions, alerts, border incidents, and naval
clashes over the Shatt al-Arab, the vital waterway
that is in dispute between the two countries. On
September 22, 1980, Iraq, after extensive air raids
deep into Iran, finally launched a massive land invasion, and the war was deemed officially to have
started. There had been plenty of warning.

The immediate international reaction to the war
was confused. The Soviets blamed the countries of
the West, saying that they had instigated the Iraqi
attack for profit. The United States, which was

in the midst of the hostage crisis with Iran, called for international restraint but not for any action. Secretary-General Kurt Waldheim immediately appealed to both sides, offered his good offices, and demanded an urgent meeting of the Security Council. The council took four days before it actually held a formal meeting—an extraordinary display of apathy at the beginning of a major war.

Two days later, the Security Council passed a resolution that called for restraint, a cease-fire, peaceful settlement, and the acceptance of mediation, but failed to refer to the country which had been the prime mover in the war—namely Iraq— or to demand the withdrawal of Iraqi troops from Iranian territory. This, not surprisingly, infuriated the government of Iran.

At the outset Iraq was confident of early victory and had no wish to be told by the Security Council to stop. Iran believed that it had been betrayed by the international community, and therefore had no wish to ask for help.

What should have happened? The UN Charter sets out a clear sequence of moves which are supposed to govern a situation of this kind. The member states, in signing the Charter, had agreed to settle their disputes by peaceful means and refrain from the threat or use of force. The Security Council has a primary responsibility for the maintenance of international peace and order. The member states are supposed to seek a solution to their difficulties by negotiation, inquiry, mediation, or any other peaceful means they wish to choose.

If member states fail to comply with these rules, perhaps because one or the other of them wants to seize an opportunity to gain some advantage or to settle some old score by force, the Security Council machinery is supposed to come into action. The council has a responsibility to investigate international disputes in order to determine whether they are a threat to the wider peace; certainly the Gulf War, in an area of great strategic importance, was such a threat. The council may then intervene to recommend means of settlement. If that fails, the council, under Chapter 7 of the Charter, can impose economic or other sanctions and even use military force in an effort to put an end to the hostilities. In the early days of the United Nations, the possibility of using sanctions and even military force was the part of the Charter that attracted most attention. It was called the "teeth" of the Charter. The fact is that, largely because of East-West disagreement, these teeth have never been put in place, let alone used.

Apart from moves by the Security Council itself, any member of the United Nations can bring a situation to the Security Council for its consideration. The Secretary-General also has the right to bring a situation to the attention of the council under Article 99 of the Charter, if he believes that situation to be a threat to international peace. In fact, Secretary-General Waldheim did just that in 1980 with the Iran-Iraq War, unfortunately with no serious effect. Normally the Security Council acts only on the instigation of a member state or of the Secretary-General.

A number of factors determine what happens or doesn't happen in the Security Council—the interests of the five permanent members of the council; the interests of the other members; and the nature of the dispute and the interests of the parties who are engaged in it. Action, therefore, is not automatic.

What were the various motivations in the Iran-Iraq case? Iraq was certainly alarmed by the Iranian Revolution, which had sent out shock waves all over the area. Iraq was particularly concerned with Ayatollah Khomeini's appeal to the Shi'a of Iraq, who constitute some 65 percent of the Iraqi population, to give their allegiance to Iran. The relationship between the two rulers could hardly have been worse. In 1978, at the request of the Shah, President Sadam Hussein of Iraq had expelled Khomeini from Iraq, where he had taken refuge. This was the reason why Khomeini went to Paris, where he was much better situated to promote the Iranian Revolution.

The Iraqi aim was presumably a quick and bold military strike to neutralize—a polite word for "topple"—the Iranian revolutionary government. If this move had succeeded speedily, it would not have been unpopular in the Arab world, nor, in all probability, in countries farther afield. Iraq, perhaps influenced by exiled Iranian generals, evidently thought that Iran would be a military pushover. It seems unlikely that the dispute between Iran and Iraq over the Shatt al-Arab was the basic reason for Iraq to go to war, and in fact the Iraqis raised this issue only as a kind of justification after they had already invaded Iran. In any case, Iraq had absolutely no reason or wish to take its problems to the Security Council. Iraq wanted to get the war over quickly before it could be interfered with.

Iran also had no reason or inclination to go to the Security Council over its differences with Iraq. Iran had evoked the unanimous disapproval of the council over its holding of the American hostages. It therefore tended to see the Security Council as a tool of the US State Department. The Secretary-General had also been much concerned with the hostage business. He had invoked Article 99 to bring the problem to the council and had been to Tehran in an attempt to get the hostages released. He also was not particularly popular with Iran. Iran didn't trust the United Nations and didn't want to resort to it.

As far as the superpowers were concerned, this was a period of bad Soviet-US relations, which had recently been worsened by the Soviet operation in Afghanistan. There was therefore no realistic possibility of the two superpowers getting together to nip the Iran-Iraq War in the bud. The Soviets were interested in improving their somewhat shaky relations with the revolutionary government of Iran at a time when that government was in a state of anti-American fervor. At the same time, the Soviets had a treaty of friendship with Iraq, which they had provided with the bulk of its armaments, so they did not want to rock the boat with Iraq either. Thus the Soviets were not likely to take a strong public position about the war, except to accuse the West of starting it.

The United States had no diplomatic relations with either country, and therefore very limited influence, quite apart from the hostage crisis. The United States at that time was also extremely sensitive to further Soviet moves in the area after the invasion of Afghanistan. Rumors were rife about the Soviet quest for warm-water ports and the possibility of Soviet forces pressing on south through Pakistan. Although it did not get most of its own oil from the Gulf, the United States was also concerned about a situation which might jeopardize the oil supplies of its main allies. Thus, the United States made general appeals but did not urge or try to promote any sort of concerted action.

In the international community there was a generally negative feeling toward Iran, and therefore little enthusiasm for active involvement to stop Iraq. The general wish seemed to be that the war would end, and end quickly. France especially was very close to Iraq both militarily and economically.

In general, governments were nervous about one another's motivations—economic, military, and political. Such an atmosphere is not conducive to the kind of effective concerted action envisaged in the Charter. In other words, a mood of expediency overrode respect for the principles of the UN Charter. Not for the first time, mutual suspicions and short-term national interests proved to be much stronger forces than principles or the long-term common interest of avoiding a very serious threat to international peace and order. The war went relentlessly on.

As mentioned earlier, the Security Council did not meet until September 26, four days into the war, and two days later it passed a resolution calling for a cease-fire, but making no reference either to Iraqi aggression or to the withdrawal of Iraqi forces from Iranian territory, an omission that ensured that Iran would not take the council seriously in the future.

As frequently happens in such situations, the Security Council soon passed the buck to the Secretary-General, who appointed the distinguished Swedish politician Olof Palme as his special representative. Palme first tried to find out whether there was any common ground between the two fighting countries for some kind of settlement. He came to the conclusion that there wasn't, and therefore decided that the only thing to do was to tackle particular problems. For example, a number of ships were trapped by the war in the Shatt al-Arab. Palme's efforts to get them out were finally defeated by Iraq's insistence that the arrangements must recognize its sovereignty over the disputed waterway. Other efforts included trying to stop attacks on civilian targets and to get better conditions for prisoners of war.

In retrospect it seems that there might have been a slim possibility of getting a cease-fire in 1982. In that year Iraq had been pushed back to its own borders, and Iran had not yet begun to insist that Iraq must be indicted as an aggressor and that Iraq's president, Sadam Hussein, must step down before Iran would agree to stop fighting. The foreign minister of Algeria, who had negotiated the treaty between Iran and Iraq in 1975, was at this time mediating between the two belligerents. That effort came to a tragic end when the foreign minister's plane was shot down by mistake by an Iraqi fighter with an air-to-air missile. With him and his entire staff perished the records and the hope of his negotiations. Algeria at that time enjoyed the confidence of both sides.

The Security Council finally met again in 1982, after two years of inactivity, but nothing really happened. The Secretary-General continued submitting plans and suggestions to the parties and trying to deal with particular problems, with some limited success. There was a truce on attacks on civilian targets in 1983–1984. The introduction of chemical warfare, a matter of grave international concern, was investigated and reported on.

The problem of a cease-fire remained. Iraq wanted an immediate cease-fire and withdrawal of Iranian troops, the Iranians now being the invaders. Iran refused to negotiate with Sadam Hussein and wanted an international indictment of Iraq for aggression before agreeing to a cease-fire. The war continued and spread. Tanker traffic in the Gulf became a target for both sides. Iran's greatest offensive, against Basra, started in December 1986.

It was at this stage that in January 1987 the Secretary-General, as previously noted, called on the permanent members of the Security Council to put their authority behind a new effort to end the war. There was a very complex negotiation for six months on the text of a Security Council resolution, which was finally adopted unanimously on July 20, 1987, as Resolution 598. As such international resolutions usually do, Resolution 598 looked good on paper. It was under Articles 39 and 40, the enforcement part of the Charter. It demanded an end to the war, and signaled that the parties could expect follow-up action by the council. It demanded a cease-fire and immediate withdrawal to national boundaries. UN observers were to verify and supervise the withdrawal and the release of prisoners of war. The Secretary-General was to mediate the terms of a comprehensive settlement of all the differences between the two countries. All other states were asked to refrain from escalating the conflict. Finally, the resolution required the Secretary-General to consult the parties on setting up an impartial body to inquire into responsibility for the conflict, thus publicly recognizing for the first time, although in the most cautious terms, that Iran had a justifiable grievance over what had happened in 1980. The resolution ended with a muffled threat of sanctions, by stating that the Security Council would meet again to consider further steps.

This unanimous agreement was widely hailed as a great achievement, and it certainly was better than nothing, and better late than never. It was also hailed as a revival of a sense of common purpose in international affairs and of the particular responsibilities of the permanent members of the Security Council.

The reality was that the responsibility had once again been passed to the Secretary-General. Neither Iran nor Iraq actually rejected Resolution 598. They simply had diametrically opposed views as to how it was going to be put into effect. Iraq maintained that it was meant to be implemented in the order of its paragraphs—that is that the cease-fire and the withdrawal of troops must take place before anything else. Iran insisted that responsibility for the war was the fundamental problem and, along with reparations, would have to be discussed first. At this time Iran still seemed to hold the offensive on the battlefield. After a lull in July and August, the ground war, the missile attacks, and the attacks on tankers started up again. By this time, the naval forces of the United States and several Western European countries were involved in protecting tankers in the Gulf, which added another element of tension to an already tense situation.

The Secretary-General submitted a new plan to Iran and Iraq, trying to get common ground between the two countries, at least enough to get a cease-fire. The issue of sanctions and an arms embargo on Iran had been kept alive by the United States, and in December 1987 efforts began in the Security Council, led by the United States, to draw up a second resolution—this time imposing sanctions on anyone who would not heed Resolution 598. This was generally taken to mean Iran. Not only the Soviet Union and China, but also countries which had important economic relations with Iran, like Japan, West Germany, or Italy, were dubious about sanctions.

The war dragged on, but Iraq now gained the military initiative and recaptured virtually all the territory it had lost to Iran. On July 3, 1988, an Iranian civilian airliner was shot down by accident by a US naval vessel with the loss of 298 lives. On July 17 Iran unexpectedly announced that it accepted a cease-fire and Resolution 598. It was now Iraq's turn to be intransigent, but after intensive efforts by the Secretary-General a cease-fire, supervised by 350 UN Military Observers, came into effect in August 1988. Under the Secretary-General's auspices negotiations began regarding the other points of Resolution 598. In the preliminary rounds Iraq's insistence on its sovereignty over the Shatt al-Arab proved to be a major obstacle, but the cease-fire held. The negotiations continue.

The Iran-Iraq War, and the efforts to deal with it, raise many important questions. Would a much firmer stance by the Security Council at the beginning have brought an early end to the war? Would an arms embargo and an embargo on the purchase of oil have made a difference, and could they have been effectively imposed? If the present, improved international climate had prevailed at the beginning of the war in 1980, would it have made a difference to the Security Council's efforts? Will the Iran-Iraq experience cause the members of the Security Council to take a tougher line at an early stage in future cases?

The practical possibility of jointly exerting real international authority—not just drafting resolutions, but actually stopping wars—is evidently still extremely limited. It is limited mainly, as I mentioned, by mutual suspicions, short-term national concerns, and the unwillingness of governments to become involved in dangerous situations. Only an international consensus on taking forceful, practical steps might have made a difference at the beginning, or indeed have made Resolution 598 into a reality when it was first adopted. That consensus did not exist.

Is it naïve to expect governments—and especially the permanent members of the Security Council—to give threats to international peace priority over their own mutual suspicions and concerns? This is what the Charter appears to expect of them. If great powers do not accept this responsibility, it is unlikely that the international community will be able to mount the kind of effort that could halt a regional war. A divided Security Council's effort will inevitably be half-hearted and will be easily deflected by the belligerents playing off one group of countries in the Security Council against another.

What degree of disaster will make governments relearn the main lesson of World War II: that there must be some degree of international authority for maintaining peace if the world is to be kept reasonably safe from the danger of escalating conflict? After forty years the essential respect for the Security Council's authority has been badly eroded. In 1948, it was possible for the Council to order a cease-fire in the first Arab-Israeli War and have that order immediately obeyed. That would be unlikely to happen now, and it may take a long time to reach that point again.

What is the international community to do with a country that believes that it is under a dangerous threat from another country? If the Security Council can't protect it, does the council have the right to tell that country that it cannot use force? Did the council have the right to tell the Israelis that, although they believed the Iraqi reactor might eventually produce weapons-grade plutonium, they could not bomb it? Did the council have the right to tell the Iraqis that, although they believed the Ayatollah was trying to destabilize their country, they could not go in and try to do something about it? This is one of the great problems of the system. As long as there is no reliable international authority on which governments can depend, it is going to be very difficult to restrain governments which believe that their security is threatened.

If we are going to deal with the agenda for the future—the global agenda of the environment and pressing economic and social matters—we are going to have to learn how to establish some tolerable degree of international peace and order. For governments to guarantee their security entirely by their own efforts is impossibly expensive and inevitably disruptive of international stability. Moreover it is a prohibitive burden on energy and resources which should be being devoted to other ends which will, in the long run, be decisive for the future. It is therefore essential that governments embrace the principle of collective security and collective responsibility, and commit themselves to developing an international system which works and can be relied on. Otherwise we shall be doomed to repeat, with our new capacity for destruction, the mistakes of the past.

Afterword

Since the first three months of 1988, when these lectures were delivered, international events have moved fast, and for the most part in an encouraging direction. The Moscow summit and the conclusion of the INF Treaty appear to have opened a new and positive period in United States–Soviet relations. The Soviet Union, under an agreement negotiated by the United Nations Secretary-General, is withdrawing its forces from Afghanistan. A cease-fire, again under an agreement negotiated by the Secretary-General, has put an end to eight years of fighting between Iran and Iraq. Progress has been made toward the ending of fighting in Angola, and the independence of Namibia seems once again to be a possibility. Here again the basic course of action is set out in a Resolution of the United Nations Security Council. Under the good offices of the Secretary-General, the leaders of the two communities in Cyprus have resumed talks on a settlement. A United Nations–sponsored solution for the Western Sahara question also appears to be in sight, and there are promising developments over the future of Cambodia.

In the encouraging light of these events, it is tempting to speculate that the Security Council is beginning to at last assume its intended role as a collegial body exercising responsibility for the common security and the good of the entire international community. If this proves to be true, the work of international organizations could take on an entirely new meaning and significance in the evolution of international order. The Security Council, as the custodian of international peace, might become convincing enough for nations to entrust their problems to it rather than engaging in the desperate and often disastrous unilateral efforts which have hitherto proved so disruptive. It might even be possible at last to tackle the boundary disputes and the time bomb of artificially created borders, the bitter legacy which colonialism bequeathed to a number of new states in Africa and elsewhere. Preemptive steps to prevent disputes from degenerating into violent conflict might also now be possible.

The current positive trend is symptomatic of a resurgence of common sense in the relations between governments—of a realization that the concerns and challenges that unite humanity are far more important than the issues which divide it. It seems that the fact of interdependence is at last being recognized on the political level. If this trend gains strength it should be possible to begin to use and develop the United Nations as it was intended to be used—as an instrument for cooperation and collective responsibility. Heaven knows there is enough in our overcrowded world to be cooperative and responsible about.

The world is now faced with a new and pressing agenda—a variety of global problems which have a vital bearing on the future. The very concept of international security is of necessity being expanded to include the environmental security of the planet itself. To free the energy and resources necessary to tackle these problems will require a major cooperative effort by all governments. If the present encouraging trend is indeed the direction of the future, the revolution of decolonization will take its place in history as an essential step toward a real international community of states. That community alone can hope to achieve the world of peace, stability, and justice of which humanity has so long dreamed.

Appendix A. The United Nations System and the Future

(Delivered as the Martin Wight Memorial Lecture at the Royal Institute of International Affairs, Chatham House, London, September 27, 1988)

To be invited to give this fourteenth Martin Wight Memorial Lecture is a great honor. Martin Wight was a scholar and an internationalist who saw international relations as an effort to achieve a balance between anarchy and the common interest. Believing as he did that the community of interests of states would hold international organizations together to act for the common good, he tended to be disillusioned with the League of Nations and its successor, the United Nations.

Martin Wight was a perceptive student and writer on the concept of international authority and international security. Sir Michael Howard, who delivered a previous lecture in this series, refers to "the moral force which he brought to intellectual questions" and to his realization of the crushing responsibilities of statesmen in an infinitely complex world. Martin Wight saw international relations as a human predicament to be analyzed and understood, but his work seems to have led him to be fundamentally pessimistic about international organization. I wonder what he would have made of the situation today.

If I had been giving this lecture two years ago I would probably have adopted a somewhat wistful tone of "what might have been" and "what on earth can we do now." I might have mentioned Secretary-General Pérez de Cuellar's 1982 annual report on making the United Nations, and especially the Security Council, work better and have said that it was a pity that the Security Council had been unable to act on it. I would have referred to the necessity of unanimity and of East-West cooperation in the face of threats to the peace. I would have spoken of the dream, apparently never to be realized, of a collegial Security Council rising above national preoccupations to fight for the common good. I would have referred to the desirability of preemptive international action to prevent disputes from developing into conflicts. I would have extolled the desirability of fact-finding to establish the real situation in incipient conflicts. I would have suggested means of strengthening peacekeeping. I would have urged that governments not rest on their laurels when they had managed to agree on the text of a resolution, but that they follow up that resolution with all the support necessary to make it a reality. I would have urged the diminishing of rhetoric and the use of the United Nations less for confrontation and more for cooperation on difficult problems. I might have expressed regret that in an age of revolutionary change old political relationships and problems so far had prevented the recognition of the undoubted fact of interdependence.

In other words, I would have pronounced a lament for forty years of tiptoeing around the Cold

War and especially around the obstructions of Soviet policy. I might have tried to revive my own spirits and those of the audience by talking of what had been achieved by people simply doing what they could in an inclement international climate and impossible political conditions, and of how it was surprising that so much had been achieved.

The effectiveness of the United Nations is mainly determined by two factors, the international climate and the way governments choose to use the organization. There is now an extraordinary change in both of these conditions. We hear no more talk of the "evil empire" and, instead of Soviet negative rhetoric and blocking tactics, we have a veritable cornucopia of neo-internationalist Soviet proposals. "A change that is cause for shaking the head in wonder is upon us . . . the prospect of a new age of world peace. The United Nations has an opportunity to live and breathe and work as never before." You may think that I am quoting the chairman of the United Nations Association. Actually it is President Reagan, addressing the General Assembly yesterday (September 26, 1988).

There seems to be a sudden, dazzling outburst of common sense among governments. This trend seems to date from early 1987 when the permanent members of the Security Council got together, at the suggestion of the Secretary-General, to consider what could be done about the Iran-Iraq War. General Secretary Gorbachev, in his famous article on Soviet international policy which appeared in *Pravda* and *Izvestia* in September 1987, helped to set the tone.

Why are we so persistent in raising the question of a comprehensive system of international peace and security? Simply because it is impossible to put up with the situation in which the world has found itself on the threshhold of the third millennium—in the face of a threat of annihilation, in a state of constant tension, in an atmosphere of suspicion and strife, spending huge funds and quantities of work and talent of millions of people, only to increase mutual mistrust.

Since that time Soviet representatives have produced a continual spate of ideas. What is remarkable is not so much the novelty of such ideas, many of which have often been put forward by people in the West, but the fact that the Soviets have put them forward at all. The Soviets have urged, for example, a more active and independent role for the Secretary-General. They have suggested a far greater degree of international verification in different areas of activity. They have suggested that peacekeeping would be greatly strengthened by central training and logistics institutions. They have extolled the merits of independent fact-finding, something that they have bitterly opposed in the past. They have suggested the resurrection of the Military Staff Committee, consisting of the chiefs of staff of the five permanent members, which has been more or less inactive since 1946 but was originally hailed as the "teeth" of the United Nations. They have suggested that the purely intergovernmental institutions of the United Nations system are not enough and that they should be paralleled by some form of nongovernmental system representing the people of the world. They have talked about the desirability of an international intellectual commission to give a voice in world affairs to the world's most creative people.

In listening to all this one sometimes feels like pinching oneself, but there is no question that the international climate has become clement in a way that it has not been since 1945. On top of this the countries of the Third World, after all the rhetoric and radicalism of the 1970s and early '80s, have become pragmatic, unideological, cooperative, mature, and constructively self-critical. The net result is that conditions for international activity are more promising than at any time since 1945.

This great change has already had some practical results. Soviet forces are leaving Afghanistan under an arrangement negotiated by the United Nations. Iran and Iraq have ceased hostilities under a cease-fire agreement negotiated by the Secretary-General of the United Nations. The parties to the problem of Western Sahara have accepted in principle the Secretary-General's proposal for a settlement. The leaders on the island of Cyprus have gone back to the negotiating table under the good offices of the Secretary-General and have promised to report on their discussions in the early future. There are signs that the problems of Namibia and Angola may be on their way to a satisfactory settlement and that the independence process for Namibia may shortly commence under United Nations supervision. There are a number of negotiations going on in order to try to deal with the problems of Cambodia and its neighboring states.

Is it really time to proclaim the "renaissance" of the United Nations? This seems to be the mood in some sections of the media which in the past have not been slow to pronounce the United Nations dead. It would be wise, I think, to react rather cautiously to the current developments. The UN, although the media seldom remember it, has had periods of enthusiasm and success before, under Dag Hammarskjold in the fifties, for example, not to mention the euphoric atmosphere which attended the organization's birth in 1945. As late as 1973 the UN's actions in bringing an end to the Middle East war were hailed as a vindication and a great success for the organization. In fact, a sober assessment of the UN's forty-three-year history would show a lot of positive developments—developments, incidentally, which have prepared the ground for the present positive situation. The peaceful conclusion of the process of decolonization, the development of human rights as a priority item on the agenda of the international community, the massive promulgation of international law, are all general developments of permanent importance. Attention to great global problems such as the environment, population, food, migration, water, and many others has been a notable feature of the United Nations system's business since the early 1970s. The negotiation of the Treaty on the Law of the Sea is an outstanding example of the capacity of the international community to tackle an immensely complex problem by negotiation and consensus. It is to be hoped that the ideological objections to the treaty by the three powers which have held out against ratifying it—the United States, Britain, and West Germany—may soon be overcome. There have been great strides in international action for disadvantaged groups of people, in disaster relief, and in dealing with problems of refugees. The international machinery on the drug problem is now being mobilized as never before.

On the peace and security side, although the Security Council has hitherto been unable to function to its full power as envisaged in the Charter, effective methods of conflict control and negotiation have been improvised, and the council has a long record of suggesting the comprehensive terms of settlement for a number of very difficult problems. The technique of peacekeeping, a complete innovation thirty years ago, has become an accepted practice. The new climate may well give it a chance to grow into a far more broadly effective institution.

All in all the international community, during forty very difficult years, has demonstrated some of the possibilities of collective responsibility and of cooperative management of global problems. We are now beginning to reap the harvest of all this hard and mostly unacclaimed work.

Secretary-General Javier Pérez de Cuellar summed up the present juncture well in his current annual report on the work of the organization.

> The developments of the past months have not been fortuitous. They are the result of diplomatic activity sustained over the years by the United Na-

tions and intensified recently. On matters of international peace and security, the principal organs of the United Nations have increasingly functioned in the manner envisaged in the Charter. The working relationship of the Security Council and the Secretary-General has rarely if ever been closer. I am thankful for this as also for the recent improvement in international relations at the global level that has opened new possibilities for successful action by the world body. Multilateralism has proved itself far more capable of inspiring confidence and achieving results than any of its alternatives. Millions around the world have had a gratifying demonstration of the potential of the organization and the validity of the hopes they place in it.

I do not think the time has yet come for too much self-congratulation either by governments or by international organizations. In fact, we are just getting in sight of the starting line on which we all believed we were in 1945. The conditions are unprecedentedly favorable, but there is still a very long way to go.

Let me illustrate what I mean by posing a number of questions. On the peace and security side, for example, will the Security Council be able, as the custodian of international peace, to inspire enough confidence for nations to entrust their security to it rather than going it alone in often disastrous unilateral adventures? Will the renunciation of force in international relations and the peaceful settlement of disputes—two basic principles of the United Nations Charter—become the reality in governmental policies? Will the new climate affect really difficult problems such as the Israel-Arab-Palestinian problem? What about the original Charter concept of collective security leading progressively to disarmament? In 1945, after six years of world war, this seemed eminently sensible, but we don't hear very much about that concept today. Is it still a long-term objective of governments? Is the steady progress toward the rule of law in international affairs still a basic objective of the governments of the world? What effective role will the United Nations be able to play in the vast economic and social problems which all countries, in different degrees, now face?

These are some of the questions we need to ask before we get carried away by the current tide of optimism. It seems possible that the necessity for collective responsibility for international peace and security is now coming into focus, but it would certainly be premature to entertain the notion that war as an instrument of international policy is going out of style.

Such a development would be eminently desirable and might be coming about just in time, for while we are resting in the new sunshine of global détente, a new and mighty range of problems looms before us. The economic problems facing the world, and especially the developing countries, are formidable enough in themselves. Debt, burgeoning poverty and population, and rampant social decay are only some of the phenomena which, if not checked and remedied, can only produce increasing instability. Environmental problems are intricately related to other developments, and we now appear to be facing a serious man-made threat to the sustaining balance of nature which has preserved us since the dawn of time. The very concept of international security must now be expanded to include the environmental security of the planet itself.

Most of these so-called global problems can only be tackled by major cooperative efforts by all the governments and peoples of the world. Such efforts will require energy and resources on a scale which demands that conventional conflicts, which have hitherto absorbed so much of our attention and resources, be treated far more effectively by the international community. Governments have not only to accept the fact of interdependence— that much overused word—but also to act on it, and act cooperatively. Some Soviet representatives have said that this is a basic reason for the radical change in Soviet international policy. Surprisingly enough, at the moment we seem to be in a better position to move ahead on the peace and security side of international life than on the economic or environmental side.

The current mood of optimism may serve to remind both governments and the public that we already have a basic international framework in the United Nations, its specialized agencies and programs, and the various regional organizations. It may not be the best or most effective design, but it is a basis, and it is the only one we have. We now need to get this machinery going, and to improve, revitalize, and modify it as the situation so obviously demands.

What sorts of changes are required to update the international machinery and make it more effective? This is a vast subject, and the following suggestions are merely random samples.

The mechanism of the Security Council has already undergone an extraordinary transformation, with the permanent members consistently cooperating to consider the problems before the council, something that they have not done since the UN's inception. The original idea of a collegial Security Council dealing with problems of peace and security for the common good, rather than on the basis of individual national interest, now for the first time seems to be a possibility. I mentioned earlier various suggestions that it may now be possible to make use of the Military Staff Committee. The Military Staff Committee was to consist of the chiefs of staff of the five permanent members, and was to assist the council not only on military and enforcement matters but also on general questions such as disarmament. The international climate may now be right for the revitalization of this body. It could perhaps also be used for new tasks such as providing a more consistent and adequate logistical basis for United Nations peacekeeping operations, which have hitherto tended to be conducted on a logistical shoestring of improvisation and good luck.

Peacekeeping itself has taken on a new lease on life. This invaluable technique requires the full support of the Security Council, the cooperation, however grudging, of the parties in conflict, and a rigorously correct use and direction of the operation. Adequate funds and logistical support and the availability of suitable troops are also vital. The new climate may make it possible to enhance these essential prerequisites as never before. If so, peacekeeping may take its place as a historic step toward the principle of nonviolence in international relations.

It may be possible now to change the approach to the negotiation of difficult problems. Hitherto negotiations have tended to start from zero with long discussions of procedure and to degenerate into counterproductive bargaining. If a benevolent international consensus could set forth the outline of the final objectives of negotiations on difficult problems, it might be possible to structure the negotiations themselves in a more focused and positive way.

It is worth considering why the notion of international mediation has been largely moribund since the mid-sixties. Count Bernadotte, who was assassinated in 1948, was the last person to have the temerity to put forward a comprehensive plan for a settlement of the Palestine problem. In fact this cost him his life. Perhaps the climate is ripe for international mediation to take the stage once again.

The introduction of the rule of law has always been regarded, in theory at any rate, as a desirable basic development in international relations. One way to encourage this development would be a far greater tendency by governments to bring justiciable cases of international disputes to the International Court of Justice instead of letting them become political footballs between countries. It would follow, of course, that governments would get into the habit of abiding by the findings of the International Court.[1]

In the Law of the Sea Treaty, the Seabed Authority provides a model for developing international authority over important parts of humanity's common heritage. The Seabed Authority has been objected to in some countries, including the United Kingdom, as a quasi-socialistic measure. On the other hand, it is unquestionably clear that a far greater degree of international management and authority is going to be required if humanity's common heritage is not to be recklessly expended in a way which will bequeath to our grandchildren a series of irreversible problems. This is a debate which should be urgently pursued.

The problems now facing humanity require more than a routine diplomatic or political reaction. If we are to hope to solve them and restore the word "progress" to our vocabulary, intellect and technology will have to be mobilized to work in tandem with intergovernmental organizations. The European Commission has shown the way in which this can be done on a regional scale. It would seem that the international conditions may now allow a far greater degree of intellectual and technological cooperation in the world at large than has been practicable hitherto.

The idea of a parallel public and nongovernmental international network to push for support for international programs, to bring nongovernmental concerns to the fore, and to raise public consciousness is by no means a new idea. The United Nations has run a number of conferences with parallel nongovernmental conferences: the environment conference in Stockholm in the early seventies, for example, and the conference on the status of women in Nairobi in the early 1980s. The setting up of such a parallel network on a broader scale might well give international organizations the vitality, the human factor, and the responsiveness they have tended to lack.

The strains of the East-West relationship have posed major obstacles to good organization and administration in the United Nations system. To take only one example, the political conditions have made it impossible hitherto to consider whether the Secretary-General might have one or two deputies to relieve the enormous burden of a job which is, in fact, three or four full-time jobs The objection has been that it is difficult to get general agreement on one top international civil servant, and to get agreement on more than one would be politically impossible. It seems conceivable now that this obstacle to good leadership and organization may have been at least significantly reduced.

These are just a few of the practical possibilities which may now be opening up. There are certainly many more, but to get tangible results will require a great deal of work. It will also require leadership of the highest order, commitment by governments to principles and to long-term goals, and a new degree of consistency and common sense in using international organizations. Only better and more flexible organization and innovative ideas will provide the international capacity to adjust with success to the enormous changes that are now taking place worldwide.

Inevitably, such an adjustment will cut across national sovereignty and the short-term interests of nations. The question is whether a sense of collective responsibility will overcome such obstacles and make progress possible. Such advances will require a far greater involvement of an informed public and a far higher level of intellectual stimulus than has been the case until now. If we are to go forward to a successful readjustment of our international system, we need to involve the Martin Wights of this world as well as politicians, diplomats, and technocrats.

In the brief euphoria of 1945 the United Nations was conceived of as a sort of Pax Victoriosa. Looking back we can see that much of the orientation of the organization was a retrospective attempt to deal with the problems of the 1930s in a way which governments had significantly failed to do at the time. Unfortunately the political conditions quickly soured, and what had seemed a dream about to be realized was soon forgotten or derided as an unrealistic flight of postwar idealism.

After forty-three very hard years of revolutionary turmoil and change, there is a new international atmosphere and a new chance, but the basic problem remains the same. Ralph Bunche identified it in 1946: "Building an international order in which freedom, justice, and mutual respect shall prevail is a slow and tortuous business. With nations, as with people, organized effort is needed to induce them to live and get along together in community."

We have a new opportunity which is also a tremendous challenge. I hope that the organized effort which Bunche mentioned can at last be freed from the cynicism and flat-earthism about international organizations and international co-operation which has been so notable in the past. What is needed is a period of measured and well-informed enthusiasm. We are moving in the right direction, but almost everything else remains to be done.

Appendix B. The Future of Peacekeeping

(Delivered as the Cornelis Van Vollenhoven Memorial Lecture, Leiden University, the Netherlands, November 22, 1988; published in Negotiation Journal 5, no. 1 [January 1989]; reprinted by permission of Plenum Publishing Corporation)

For someone who has spent his whole career in the quest for international order and stability it is a particular honor and pleasure to be giving this lecture. Professor Cornelis Van Vollenhoven was a farsighted disciple of Grotius. He wrote and spoke, three-quarters of a century ago, of many things which have now come to pass. He foresaw with outstanding clarity the needs of the community of nations if it was going to live in peace.

Already in 1916, in the middle of World War I, Van Vollenhoven was writing about peace and international police. He quoted Andrew Carnegie, speaking in the Hague Peace Palace in 1913 of an "entente of three or four principal civilized nations," acting in concert against the disturbers of world peace. Van Vollenhoven suggested a "permanent international board of naval and military officers to organize the joint forces." His idea was "to convert the military cooperation of today, as instanced by the Entente and the Central Powers, intended collectively to threaten, into a new cooperation, intended collectively to protect."[1]

Van Vollenhoven foreshadowed the UN Charter in many ways, and especially as to the intended role of the Security Council and its Military Staff Committee. He was a tireless protagonist of the rule of law among nations.

He was also a witty and perceptive writer. In 1925, in "Grotius and Geneva," he describes a phenomenon very familiar to anyone who has tried to make international organizations work.

> The mind of the Geneva assembly time and again was the mind of Grotius. Yet when the delegates returned to their countries, great or small countries, they were told by their foreign offices, great or small—righteous men, peaceful men, considerate men—that they had been led astray over there by visionaries, by idealists;—that the "experience of the history of all times"—notice the momentous words "the experience of the history of all times"— teaches careful men that Karneades and Hobbes were right and Grotius was wrong.[2]

Personally, I have always been a Grotius man *and* an idealist. All my experience, in war and in peace, has only served to confirm that, in international as in national affairs, the rule of law is an essential ultimate objective for a society which wishes to survive in reasonable conditions. Furthermore I am convinced, more than ever, that idealism, which is the distillation of human experience, is far more realistic than ideology, let alone cynicism or defeatism. In my experience, self-styled realists tend to land themselves and everyone else in trouble. Ideologues want to impose their ideas on everyone else. True idealists impose their convictions primarily on themselves.

It is a particular honor to be asked to give a lecture commemorating someone who was already asserting these propositions so eloquently and so forcefully in the early years of this century. And it is appropriate that such a lecture should deal with the future of peacekeeping.

What stage have we reached in the search for international peace and stability? In 1945, the great design for the future, the UN Charter, was greeted with general enthusiasm. It seemed that governments had at last learned the lessons of two world wars. There followed some forty years of poor to atrocious international weather. These were also forty years of radical change both on the international scene and, through the technological revolution, in the way people live and communicate. During this period the initial enthusiasm for the Charter evaporated, and faith in the possibility of an orderly international future was severely tested. A basic assumption of the Charter, the unanimity of the great powers in matters of peace and security, turned out to be false, and a number of ways to get around this large hole in the foundations of the world organization had to be improvised. Among these improvisations were an expansion of the role of the Secretary-General and the technique of "peacekeeping," a new concept not found in the Charter.

It says something for the basic will to peace of the world community that, in spite—or perhaps partly because—of a staggering arms race, World War III has not taken place. Indeed the United Nations Security Council has had considerable success, using the two improvisations I mentioned, in preventing regional conflicts from escalating into a confrontation between East and West. Fifteen peacekeeping operations and countless good offices missions by successive Secretaries-General have been an important part of this effort.

After forty-two stormy years, the international climate has now become unprecedentedly mild. The paralyzing rigors of the Cold War and the storms of regional conflict appear to be giving way to common sense, negotiation, and reason. The prospect of realizing the dreams of 1945, as expressed in the UN Charter, are better than at any time in forty years.

This change has come none too soon. A better system of international security and stability is urgently needed. Modern weapons technology has made war an unacceptable and inefficient anachronism. It is an anachronism, moreover, which requires preparations too expensive even for the richest and most powerful nations. Even the US and the USSR are finding this out.

The community of nations is also faced by another compelling challenge. We are now encountering a new generation of global problems which can only be faced in cooperation. Our capacity to deal with these problems will determine the nature and conditions of life on this planet in the next century. It is obviously high time to concentrate resources and political energy on this part of the international agenda. Indeed it is essential if our children and grandchildren are to live in tolerable conditions.

In dealing with both sets of issues—peace and stability and global problems—a key question will be our ability to make the instruments of collective responsibility and international authority more effective. With the abolition of great colonial empires which was one of the objectives of the Charter, we have for the first time in human history a world of independent sovereign states— over 160 of them—*not* dominated by one or two great competing empires. There is therefore an urgent need to establish an acceptable degree of international authority to regulate the affairs of this world in matters of essential common concern. On what methods and sanctions will this essential international authority rest?

As regards international peace and security, the Charter sets out a process which is based on the renunciation of the use of force in international relations and on the peaceful settlement of disputes. If these principles fail, the Charter provides for enforcement measures which the world community may take through the Security Council. These range from various forms of sanctions to the use of military forces by the Security Council. In retrospect, one may see these provisions as a belated blueprint for dealing with aggressors like Hitler and Mussolini. In the political and military conditions of the postwar world, however, the option of international enforcement has not proved to be a practical proposition.

Instead the Security Council and the Secretary-General have pioneered another route—the route of consensus, conciliation, good offices, diplo-

matic pressure, and nonviolent, cooperative peacekeeping. It is this last concept that I shall be
discussing.

The essence of peacekeeping is the use of soldiers as the catalyst for peace rather than as the
instruments of war. It is, in fact, the exact op-
posite of the military enforcement action against
aggression foreseen in Chapter VII of the Charter. International enforcement against aggressors,
which might have been effective in the special
conditions of the 1930s if the will to collective action had been present, would now seem to have
been outmoded both by the nature of international
politics and by the technological development of
warfare. While the arms race continues, against
all logic and common sense, the nations seem
again, at least in principle, to have opted tacitly
for the rule of international authority and law,
sanctioned by diplomatic pressure and persuasion.
This option is symbolized, in conflict areas, by
nonfighting soldiers, the UN's "Blue Helmets,"
whose duty is to remain above the battle and only
to use their weapons in the last resort for self-
defense. They are soldiers without enemies, even
when their clients are bellicose or resentful.

The peacekeeping route to conflict resolution
has long been championed, in principle at least,
by the nations of the West and of the nonaligned
group, even if it is, for the moment, paralleled
by another track of armaments and military alliances. In 1987, the peacekeeping route was also,
at long last, ardently embraced by the leaders of
the Soviet Union, which had hitherto been generally sceptical of, and often actively opposed to, the

concept of United Nations peacekeeping. Thus for the first time there is a virtually unanimous international constituency for promoting the concept of international authority through consensus and joint action, conciliation, diplomatic pressure, and, where necessary, peacekeeping operations to monitor and tranquilize the area of conflict.

This is an encouraging development—at least in principle. What are the prospects for its practical effectiveness in achieving peace and stability? For encouragement, we may perhaps look to the evolution of civilian police in the nation-state, a development which began in most countries in the nineteenth century. The development of civilian police as the guardians and symbols of the law and of public safety helped nation-states to cross the line from lawless factional violence to civil authority and respect for law in the common interest of all the citizens of a state.

In my own country, Great Britain, the leader of this experiment was Sir Robert Peel, who first established a police force (the "Peelers") in Ireland in 1819. Although his Irish experiment had not been well received, being viewed by nationalists and Catholics alike as an instrument of repression, he established a second police force (the "Bobbies") in England in 1829. Nor was Peel's initiative well received in England. Members of Parliament felt that the new police would infringe on the authority of local government, and working men feared the police would be used to break strikes, interfere in trade disputes, and spy on working-class political movements. The new police were variously known as "blue locusts," "lobsters," and "blue devils." (Blue seems to be the symbolic color of peacekeeping.) They were blamed for consuming tax money and producing nothing in return. They were often assaulted or greeted with hostile demonstrations. However, the support of the propertied classes, the government, and local agricultural and industrial leaders, and their desire for stability and security, won the day. Concentration on efficiency and intolerance of corruption gradually gained their acceptance from a skeptical populace. The police soon became a trusted national institution.

What were the conditions which allowed civilian police to emerge as the guardians of the law and the main protectors of public safety? First of all, a responsible central government which wished to strengthen the rule of law without resorting to repressive or violent measures. Second, the desire of the overwhelming majority of the population to move away from factional violence, disorder, and lack of security to a more peaceful and productive state of affairs. Third, the disarming of factions and the restriction of the right to bear arms to the national army only. Fourth, and perhaps most important, pride in the vision of an evolving democratic society relying on respect for the law and for the government rather than on armed might—a society taking pride in protecting the rights of the weak and limiting the power of the strong.

Is it fanciful to apply this model to the current international scene and to see the role of peacekeeping as analogous to the role of the civilian police in the national transition from factional violence and general insecurity to democratic freedom and order under the constitutional rule of law? Certainly there now seems to be a far greater interest among all governments in making the United Nations system, including the International Court of Justice, progressively more effective. Throughout the world there is a manifest fatigue and disgust with war, conflict, and violence. In this past year we have seen a number of long-standing conflicts yield to common sense, negotiation, and United Nations arrangements, of which peacekeeping operations are an important part. As regards disarmament and arms control, the situation is anything but satisfactory, but at the highest level of the arms race there has been at least some initial progress. Let us hope that this example will spread to other areas of the vast armaments extravaganza which hangs over virtually every government and every part of the world.

On the international level the vision of a world community served by an effective international system has been eclipsed for nearly forty years by ideological and other conflicts and by the friction and confusion of the revolutionary changes through which the world was passing. We may now have come to a calmer time when the main priority is to assess, assimilate, and manage the vast changes which have occurred.

Dag Hammarskjold once said that "working at the edge of the development of human society is to work on the brink of the unknown."[3] We are now very much on the "brink of the unknown." A number of developments, especially in the environmental, technological, economic, and social spheres, have recently highlighted the grim realities of interdependence and the necessity to strengthen our international institutions accordingly. On the other hand, growing international concern for the weak, for the victims of disaster and the underprivileged, is a phenomenon of which we can be proud.

What does peacekeeping—an essential concept for successfully crossing the brink of the unknown—require to succeed? First of all, a strong and supportive international consensus for peace, starting in the Security Council. This means both consistent political and diplomatic support for peacekeeping operations by governments and also the requisite financial and logistic support.

The financing of peacekeeping, at a time when several large new operations are envisaged, is an urgent matter. The present financial arrangements, or lack of them, are unreliable, put an intolerable burden on the countries which provide the troops, and are also harmful to the essential principle of collective responsibility. A much more imaginative and searching study of the financial problem is needed. The cost of peacekeeping may seem large until we consider the cost of the alternative or the historic importance of an objective such as the independence of Namibia.

Second, a peacekeeping operation must have a workable and realistic mandate which is supported in practice by the international community. The experience of UNIFIL in Lebanon in its early years, in which the Netherlands participated, to name only one example, was a shocking case of UN troops' being thrown into a situation with an inadequate mandate and inadequate political support.

Third, a peacekeeping operation must have the cooperation, however grudging, of governments and established authorities in the area of conflict. The parties to the conflict must realize from the outset that the peacekeeping operation serves their long-term interests, however reluctantly they may seem to accept it. It is their honorable pretext for peace, their ticket for a transition from war to peace without losing face.

Fourth, a peacekeeping operation must have well-disciplined, capable, and broadly representative contingents and an effective, integrated command. This command must be instructed and guided at all times by the Secretary-General and his staff to ensure its coordination with the objectives of the Security Council as well as the necessary political sensitivity. These are predominantly *political* rather than military operations. Military commanders may sometimes find this difficult to accept at first.

Fifth, the principles and method of operation must be clear and must be understood and respected by the soldiers. This particularly applies to the central military question of the use of force. Force can normally only be used in the last resort in self-defense. Experience shows that a peacekeeping operation which uses its weapons for purposes other than self-defense quickly becomes part of the conflict and therefore part of the problem. It loses its essential status as being above the conflict and its acceptability to all sides. The multinational force in Beirut was a tragic example of the failure to observe this basic rule.

Hitherto the UN has conducted fifteen peacekeeping operations. They have worked well, or less well, according to the degree in which the essential conditions have been present. The present favorable international climate affords the hope that future operations will be better supported and easier to run. The situation in the Security Council is particularly encouraging. The relationship and performance of the five permanent members has undergone a radical change in recent times. For the first time the permanent members seem to be on their way to becoming a collegial body, consulting together to evolve common approaches and solutions to questions of international peace and security, rather than using the council as a battleground for their own differences. If this trend continues, the effectiveness of the Security Council will be greatly strengthened. The formulation by the permanent members of the basis for ending the Iran-Iraq War was the first fruit of this new spirit, which was the original intention of the Charter.

The change in the attitude of the Soviet Union is particularly striking. New Soviet proposals, as regards both the development of the institution of peacekeeping *and* the wider use of such operations, seem to indicate that a major obstacle to the future development of peacekeeping has been removed. Indeed some of the new Soviet proposals, which parallel recommendations made in the past by successive Secretaries-General, indicate what immediate improvements in peacekeeping might be possible.

Recent Soviet proposals aim at seeing "the positive experience and practice of United Nations peacekeeping operations consolidated and further developed and put on a more solid legal and financial basis," so that they can be used "more extensively for the implementation of Security Council decisions as well as for the prevention of emerging armed conflicts." Specific suggestions include the use of UN personnel in situations where outside interference may be being used to destabilize a government; the establishment of UN observation posts in explosive areas of the world; the stationing of UN observers along frontiers of countries which are in fear of outside interference; the dispatch of observation and fact-finding missions; and the dispatch of military observer missions by the Secretary-General for preventing possible conflicts.[4] The Soviets also suggest establishing a reserve of military observers and armed forces and a system of training for UN service. The Soviet Union would itself consider providing military contingents and would take part in logistic support for UN operations.

These and other ideas, including suggestions for a more effective use of the International Court of Justice, reflect an extraordinary change in Soviet policy in areas where, in the past, Soviet opposition had impeded progress. The Soviet emphasis on the active role of the Secretary-General and on preventive action in conflict situations is particularly striking. It is to be hoped that other countries will react in a measured but positive way to the Soviet suggestions.

There are now new possibilities both to launch new and important peacekeeping operations—in Namibia and the Western Sahara, for example— and to strengthen the political, constitutional, legal, and practical foundations for such operations. We need to foster the organic growth of collective responsibility, international confidence, operational capacity, and respect for the operations of the United Nations. The present international climate would seem to be favorable for this growth. This could be a turning point in the long struggle, initiated by Grotius more than 350 years ago, to establish the rule of law in the affairs of nations.

In more general terms, the aim must be to strengthen the framework of international peace and security so that governments in trouble or under threat will see the advantage of bringing their problems to the United Nations rather than going it alone in unilateral efforts which require vast outlays for armaments and usually end in disaster. Only thus will the phrase "international peace and security" be given a reality which it has so far lacked.

In an even longer perspective, we are working for a time when war as an instrument of national policy will go out of fashion because it is too destructive, too expensive, and too ineffective. In this long perspective, the development of the concept of international peacekeeping operations has an essential place, just as the concept of police forces had in the development of the rule of law in nations.

Almost everything remains to be done, and the road ahead will be long and arduous. But let us take courage from Cornelis Van Vollenhoven, who wrote in 1919, "Grotius's Law of Nations stands at the door, and it knocks. For three hundred years we have let it knock. Now it is getting too strong for us. We have not yet turned the key, but the bolts have been drawn."[5]

Surely it is now time to pass through the door into the future.

Appendix C. Remarks at the Nobel Prize Banquet

(Delivered at the Grand Hotel Oslo in Oslo, Norway, December 10, 1988)

This is a happy occasion for the United Nations family and particularly for those—and there are many here—who have taken part in peacekeeping operations. The Nobel Peace Prize is unique among the marks of human achievement. Its award to peacekeeping operations recognizes both an important idea and all those who have, in one way or another, served it.

But this is not just a matter of satisfaction in a job well done, or of the worldwide recognition of that job which the Nobel Peace Prize represents. This occasion also helps us to realize how international institutions evolve and mature. What seems an impossible dream for one generation proves, for the next, to be an important and accepted institution.

I shall quote briefly from a speech made in the early summer of 1948. At that time the Cold War had already paralyzed the great-power unanimity and responsibility on which the United Nations Charter was supposed to be based. In Palestine, where the United Nations had crushing responsibilities, war was raging. The speaker said: "It is possible that a beginning could be made now through the establishment of a comparatively small guard force, as distinct from a striking force. . . . Such a force would have been extremely valuable to us in the past and it would undoubtedly be very valuable in the future. Even a small United Nations force would command respect, for it would have all the authority of the United Nations behind it."

The speaker was the first Secretary-General of the United Nations, Trygve Lie, speaking at Harvard University. Trygve Lie did not expect his initiative to be accepted. "The time was not ripe," he wrote in his memoirs, "for attracting the necessary governmental support. . . . They were too preoccupied with the successive measures in the Cold War . . . and with the domestic and foreign complications that all these entailed. . . . " Although Lie felt that this was a lost opportunity, United Nations military observers, the genesis of peacekeeping, were in fact first used at that time in Palestine. The seeds were already planted, even if the international weather was too cold and stormy for the crop to grow and ripen.

Forty years later the situation has greatly improved. Indeed the time seems to be ripe for the full realization of the idea Trygve Lie sketched out forty years ago. Even in the uncertain political climate of the last forty years, the need to stop wars and to control conflict in sensitive areas of the world has allowed peacekeeping to develop as an extremely useful weapon in the armory of peace. Peacekeeping has begun to be accepted by governments in conflict as an honorable alternative to war, as a useful pretext for peace, and as a means of moving from war to peace without losing face or risking humiliation. It has become, in many conflict situations, the essential prerequisite for negotiating a settlement.

On the military side too a whole new tradition has grown up. A new generation of soldiers have become accustomed to, and proud of, their role as the champions of peace rather than of war. United Nations peacekeepers have no enemies. Their duty is to remain above the conflict. They are on the battlefield to heal, to help, and to conciliate, not to kill. They embody the will of the world community for peace. They represent respect for international authority and law.

We seem at last to have reached a mild and sunny plateau in international relations. The rigors of the Cold War no longer paralyze the United Nations. The storms of regional conflict appear to be giving way to common sense, negotiation, and reason. Modern warfare is beginning to be recognized by governments as the disastrous, destructive, appallingly expensive anachronism we have long, in our hearts, known it to be. The interdependence of nations, brought about by the technological revolution and other developments, is beginning to be seen as the basic international reality of our time. Governments are turning—and not a moment too soon—to the challenges of the future.

Certainly there are many formidable problems ahead, but there is also more determination to cooperate in solving them than at any time in the past forty years. It even seems possible that humanity could now take the great step forward toward a community of nations dedicated, in deed as well as in word, to peace and justice, to mutual support and mutual respect.

If that proves to be true, peacekeeping operations, which you have honored with the Nobel Prize here in Oslo today, will be an essential part of the new structure of international peace and security. It will be an idea for which the time has come.

Notes

1. *The Decolonization Process*

1. Tom Slick, *The Last Great Hope* (San Antonio: Naylor, 1951).

2. "Self-Determination," *Encyclopedia Britannica* (1971), vol. 20, p. 191.

3. Quoted in William Safire, *Safire's Political Dictionary* (New York: Random House, 1978), p. 639.

4. Ralph Bunche, "Fundamental Freedoms and Non-Self-Governing Peoples," address to the Biennial Assembly of Methodist Women, Columbus, Ohio, May 1, 1946.

5. *Keesing's Contemporary Archives, 1942* (Essex, England: Longman Group), p. 5518.

6. Bunche, "Fundamental Freedoms and Non-Self-Governing Peoples."

7. Mohammed Ayoob, "Security in the Third World: The Worm about to Turn," *International Affairs* 60, no. 1 (Winter 1983–1984).

8. United Nations Charter, Preamble.

9. Mikhail Gorbachev, "The Reality and Guarantees of a Secure World," *Pravda* and *Izvestia,* September 17, 1987.

2. *The Question of Palestine*

1. Report of the British Royal Commission, July 7, 1937.

2. The Balfour Declaration was issued in the form of a letter written by the British Secretary of State for Foreign Affairs to Lord Rothschild on November 2, 1917.

3. *Decolonization in Africa: Experiences in International Responsibility*

1. Crawford Young, quoted in Prosser Gifford and William Roger Louis, *Decolonization and African Independence* (New Haven: Yale University Press, 1988), pp. xix–xx.

2. Gifford and Louis, *Decolonization and African Independence*, p. xi.

3. UN Document SG/900, March 8, 1960.

4. Quoted in Gifford and Louis, *Decolonization and African Independence*, p. xxii.

5. Gifford and Louis, *Decolonization and African Independence*, p. xxiii.

Appendix A. The United Nations System and the Future

1. Since this lecture was given, the United States has responded positively to Soviet suggestions on greater use of the International Court of Justice.

Appendix B. The Future of Peacekeeping

1. Cornelis Van Vollenhoven, *International Recht* (The Hague: Martinus Nijhoff, 1916).

2. Cornelis Van Vollenhoven, "Grotius and Geneva," in *Grotius* (Amsterdam: Martinus Nijhoff, 1925).

3. Dag Hammarskjold, Address to the University of Chicago Law School, Chicago, Ill., May 1, 1960.

4. The Soviet proposals are contained in a letter from Vladimir Petrovsky, deputy head of the Soviet delegation, to the Secretary-General, dated September 22, 1988 (United Nations Document A/43/629 of September 22, 1988).

5. Cornelis Van Vollenhoven, *The Three Stages in the Evolution of the Law of Nations* (Amsterdam: Martinus Nijhoff, 1919), p. 98.

The Distinguished Visiting Tom Slick Professorship of World Peace

◇

The Tom Slick Professorship of the University of Texas at Austin, endowed from the estate of the late Tom Slick of San Antonio, provides support for a continuing program of research, graduate education, and public enlightenment related to the study and understanding of conditions of world peace. The professorship is located in UT Austin's Lyndon B. Johnson School of Public Affairs.

In addition to teaching in the LBJ School, each Tom Slick Professor conducts either a conference or a lecture series on a peace-related topic. The lecture series on which this volume is based was the tenth such event.

The 1988 Visiting Tom Slick Professor was Brian Urquhart, former Under Secretary-General of the United Nations for Special Political Affairs. During his long and distinguished career, he was responsible for directing UN forces on thirteen different occasions in various global hotspots, including the Congo, Cyprus, the India-Pakistan border, and Lebanon. He worked closely with five UN Secretaries-General, from Trygve Lie to Javier Pérez de Cuellar, and his book about Dag Hammarskjold, as well as his memoirs, *A Life in Peace and War,* have been widely acclaimed. In 1985 he received the International Peace Academy's Distinguished Peacekeeper Award.

Mr. Urquhart has been a scholar-in-residence at the Ford Foundation since his retirement from the United Nations in 1986. As a central figure in the UN peacekeeping forces selected to receive the 1988 Nobel Peace Prize, he was in the delegation which accepted the prize during ceremonies in Norway in December 1988.